Down Sandy Lane

Down Sandy Lane

Christine Large

Down Sandy Lane
Christine Large

Published by Greyhound Self-Publishing, 2018

Designed, printed and bound by Aspect Design
89 Newtown Road, Malvern, Worcs. WR14 1PD
United Kingdom
Tel: 01684 561567
E-mail: allan@aspect-design.net
Website: www.aspect-design.net

ISBN 978-1-909219-55-7

CONTENTS

ACKNOWLEDGEMENTS

To my parents, Reg and Laura; my brother, Mike; and sister, Sandra, who are sadly no longer with us. I cherish my memories of growing up together on our little smallholding in Ryton.

To my children, Helen and Stephen, whose happy times shared with their Gran and Grampy inspired me to write these memories of my own childhood.

Special thanks to my dear friend Barbara for encouraging me to publish these stories which I wrote so many years ago.

My thanks also to Sam Old of Treyarnon Bay, Cornwall, for illustrating the front cover; to Charles Martell for writing the foreword; to my husband, Jim, for helping me put the book together; and to Nicky for proof reading.

FOREWORD

What wonderful memories Christine has recorded for posterity in this book!

In 1972 I came to live in neighbouring Brooms Green, less than a mile up Sandy Lane from Christine's parents, Reg and Laura. I remember them so well.

Mention is made of their house cow Tulip; once I sent an Old Gloucester cow called Duchess down to stay in the paddock at Moors Cottage for a spell. I also sent a Ryeland ram down but Reg didn't like him as he used to butt him from behind!

My family and I regularly walk down Sandy Lane which was such an important part of Christine's young life. I was so interested to read of how the road used to be, with its stream and ford, before the M50 tore through our landscape.

What an idyllic childhood she had, so beautifully portrayed in this book. I think it is vital that today's children read of how life used to be and indeed how much richer it was compared to today when children are tapping away on mobile phones and computers much as I am now.

Thank you, Christine, for sharing with us your magical world of years ago.

Charles Martell
Brooms Green, July 2018

INTRODUCTION

I grew up on a little smallholding called Moors Cottage in the village of Ryton, near Dymock, in northwest Gloucestershire where I lived with my parents, Reg and Laura Innes; my older brother, Michael; and younger sister, Sandra.

I was born at Moors Cottage on 29 May 1944 – Oak Apple Day – and my mother often told me that this was the hottest Whit Monday the country had experienced in thirty years.

Our little smallholding stood on high ground above the village and had views across to Ryton woods and from the upstairs windows we could see May Hill in the distance. It was approached by a narrow sandy lane with grass growing up the middle and high red sandstone banks on either side. Lovely elm trees grew on the top of the bank just below the cottage but sadly in the late 1960s these were affected by Dutch elm disease and had to be felled. The lane was known as Sandy Lane and it led from Ryton and continued on past our cottage to the small village of Brooms Green.

The times I have walked up and down that lane.

I should mention that Brooms Green is nowadays sometimes spelt as one word: Broomsgreen.

Moors Cottage was a simple red-brick cottage with a path running up to the front porch and a large vegetable garden at the side. A path ran down from the cottage to a small group of farm buildings which included cow sheds, fodder stores and pig sties. It had nearly four acres of land which was divided into small pasture fields. The little meadow immediately in front of the cottage we called The Pleck and this is where we kept the wood pile and where we would hang out the washing.

My parents were true country folk. My father came from a farming background and worked for a neighbouring farmer Dick Chew at Callow Farm or as it was known locally The Callow. Dad rented our cottage from Mr Chew and to supplement his income he kept and reared livestock on the holding.

Mum and Dad did not have a lot of money but they worked hard and were happy and contented. We were a very close and loving family and it was an idyllic childhood.

When I left home to get married my husband Jim and I along with our two young children Helen and Stephen would visit my parents at Moors Cottage most weekends. As I watched the children helping their granny in the kitchen and playing outside making mud pies and helping their grampy with the animals it was reminiscent of my own childhood. It was then that I decided to record those early memories. Whenever I had the odd hour I would sit down and put pen to paper recalling my childhood days in a series of short stories. They were then folded up and put in a box, hidden away for over forty years, until I recently came across them and was persuaded to put them together in this little book.

As you read on, I hope you will enjoy these stories and that they will give you a glimpse of country life in this part of Gloucestershire in the late 1940s and through the 1950s.

I would like to think they will also help provide a little local history and it is possible they may also trigger a few of your own similar memories.

MUM AND DAD
Some Brief Reflections

My father, Reginald Innes, was born into a farming family at Wassington Farm (otherwise known as Walsopthorn) in the Herefordshire village of Ashperton, five miles north west of the Market town of Ledbury. Dad was one of three brothers. His parents, Alfred and Ginny, lived at the farm with Dad's grandparents, Frederick and Anne Innes. His grandfather was a tenant farmer under the Canon Frome Estate.

Wassington was a very historic property with a sixteenth-century half-timbered farmhouse and I would loved to have seen it when the family were living there.

During the early years of the First World War both Dad's grandparents died and shortly after the family moved from Wassington to Welsh House Farm between Dymock and Newent.

My mother, Laura Selwyn, was born and brought up at Brand Green, near Upleadon at the Tower House which was on the edge of Madams Wood and Collinpark Wood. Here she lived with her parents William Selwyn, who was a thatcher by trade, and his wife Emily. She was one of ten brothers and sisters.

Dad working in The Pleck

The Welsh House Farm where Dad was living was only a couple of miles from Upleadon and that was when he met my mum and they eventually got married.

In the early years of their marriage, Dad worked on a farm at Leysters near Leominster, where my older brother Mike was born. A few years later they moved back to Gloucestershire to work for Mr Chew at the Callow Farm, Dymock. This is when they moved into Moors Cottage.

When Dad was not at work he spent most of his time on our smallholding tending to the animals and doing numerous other jobs.

He was a very practical man and everyone in the village knew where to come if they needed anything done especially if they were short of anything in the tool line. He always had things to hand. Nothing was ever thrown away and he had a lovely saying 'store is no sore.'

When I was little I remember Dad taking in the farm workers' boots to mend. He used a black iron shoe last and always had nails, tacks, bits of leather and laces to hand. Many an hour was spent cobbling.

He was also good at cutting men's hair and several of the men from the village would come up to our cottage to get their hair cut as the nearest barber was in Newent. In those days families in the village did not have cars and so a trip to Newent involved a two-mile bike ride to Dymock followed by a four-mile bus journey. Then there would be a wait for the bus home followed by a final two-mile bike ride. It was not so bad if they needed to go to town for other reasons and they could combine the journey to make it worthwhile. So Dad was a popular local barber and when they came for a hair cut they usually sat on a chair on the lawn with a towel over their shoulders and Dad set about his task. There was usually much chatting and they went away very satisfied.

I remember when I was young, Dad had some funny rhymes he would teach me. One went like this:

> I never felt a piece of felt
> That felt the same as that felt felt
> When first I felt the felt of that felt hat.

This was something completely stupid but we would often recite it to one another when we were doing things together like working with the animals and fixing fences.

Another thing he used to do to make me laugh was count in Welsh. The only numbers I can remember are Un, Dau, Tri, Pedwar, Pump. I suppose this was one, two, three, four, five. What happened to the rest of the numbers to ten I don't know.

Another of his little rhymes was:

Off went his jacket on –
Down went his sleeves rolled up.

Silly little things but I suppose quite funny when you are small. I don't think he would ever have been regarded as one of the Dymock Poets!

My mum had to work very hard as a young woman. As well as looking after the family she used to go out to work on the land with other women from the village.

She did a variety of seasonal work on the farm for Mr Chew. One of her jobs was helping to hoe the mangolds and sugar beet. This involved taking out the young seedlings and weeds in each row leaving healthy young plants, spaced apart the width of the hoe, which would grow into mature root crops. This was very time consuming and very tiring, often working in the heat of the day in summer months. The pay was not brilliant but every penny earned helped with much needed things for the home and perhaps a few luxuries. I remember Mum once saving up to have her hair permed – quite a thing at the time.

Mum also helped Dad with the feeding and cleaning out of our animals and an important part of her time was spent washing and packing eggs ready to go to the Egg Packing Station at nearby Staunton.

She loved gardening and was often busy in the vegetable garden.

She was never afraid of hard work but she always had time for we kids and was a wonderful mother. She

Mum with my brother Mike

was such a jolly person with an infectious laugh and everybody loved her.

I have many other memories of Mum and Dad and these will be cropping up quite a lot in the stories which follow.

I must just mention my brother Mike who was eleven years older than me and my sister and I always looked up to him. To us he was our hero and we loved him very much. In the early days Mike worked at Callow Farm with Dad. As a teenager he worked exceptionally hard and was expected to help out with jobs to be done at home.

The little stories that follow will show that as children we all had to muck in with the daily chores on the family smallholding.

OUR FIRST HOUSE COW
Milking and Butter Making

My maternal grandparents died within a few months of each other and my mother was left an inheritance of £100.

With some of this money she paid for a three piece suite for the sitting room and with the rest she paid for something which was to be a most treasured possession for my father – a cow to provide milk for the house.

The cow was bought by my father at Gloucester Cattle Market and was a Red Pole which we named Tulip.

The furniture cost £50 and the cow cost £50 so that was my mum's inheritance – gone.

Twice a day our house cow was milked by hand – early in the morning and late afternoon. My father or my brother usually did the milking but sometimes when they had to work long hours on the farm my sister Sandra and I were expected to do the afternoon milking when we arrived home from school. I did not mind doing this and at least it was one less job for my father to do when he got home from work.

At milking time the cow was called up from the meadow and let into the cow shed where she was tied up to a manger with a special head chain. She was given some food to eat called cow cake which was small compressed cubes of feed. Whilst eating she would hopefully keep her mind off milking and stand quiet making it easier to milk her.

Before starting to milk, the cow's udder and teats were washed clean and then I had to sit on a low three legged milking stool, push my head into her side and place the milk bucket firmly between my knees. Then using my thumb and fingers on each hand I would grasp two of the cow's teats and with a gentle rhythm pull and squeeze each teat until the milk squirted into the bucket. A cow has four teats and I would usually start with the two back teats and then move to the two front ones. Sometimes the cow would get restless and I had to be on the lookout in case she decided to kick the bucket over. Thankfully this did not happen very often.

Dad taught me to milk but I could never milk as fast as him. He could milk so fast that at the top of the bucket there would be a layer of froth on top of the milk.

When the milking was finished the cow's udder was washed again and a lovely white cream called Udsal was rubbed all over her teats to keep them soft and prevent them from cracking and getting an infection. The cow was let out of the cow shed and she would walk up to a big tank which was full of fresh water to have a very long drink before returning to the meadow until the next milking time.

It was now time to divide up the milk – some for the house and the rest for the calves who by this time were getting very excited and hungry in their pen. They soon drank their share from the buckets and were then ready to go to sleep for the night. After a long day at school I would walk back up to the cottage and just like the calves I was ready for tea and a good night's sleep.

During the following years this cow was joined by another couple of young cows which gave rich milk to make cream and butter for the family. My sister and I always enjoyed helping our mother with the butter making.

The milk would be put into large shallow bowls and covered with a white cloth. These were kept in the pantry which was cool. Each day the cream was skimmed off ready for butter making. We had a small butter churn into which the cream was put and the handle of the churn was turned until the butter curds formed. The curds were separated from the butter milk and washed several times. A little salt was added to the curds and then the butter was patted with wooden butter pats into golden yellow blocks. The waste butter milk was fed to the pigs.

If the weather turned humid or thundery it would affect the butter making and it was always much more difficult to form the curds.

When I was a little girl in the years following the Second World War, food commodities including milk and butter were rationed which was a great hardship for families particularly those living in the towns and cities. How lucky we were as a family to have access to a plentiful supply of our own milk and to be able to make our own butter. The same applied to eggs and meat and here again we were very fortunate to be self sufficient as you will read later.

BABY CALVES

The smallholding where I lived as a little girl was a wonderful place to grow up and looking back over the years I had a very happy and contented childhood.

We always had a house cow and I will tell you the story of the cow and her calves.

To enable cows to produce milk they have to have a calf which stimulates their bodies to give milk. We didn't have our own bull and our cow would be served by artificial insemination. This would involve a visit at the appropriate time by the man from the AI Centre.

Each year our cow would give birth to a calf and then the family would be provided with milk for the year. It took nine months for the baby calf to develop and grow inside its mother and there was always great excitement when the time drew near for the cow to calve. Sometimes if the cow calved in the daytime and we were at home from school we were allowed to see it born but more often than not it would arrive during the night when we were asleep. On the occasions when we were able to witness the birth it would not take long before the calf tried to stand up on its wobbly legs and move round to its mother's head. She would lick the calf all over and make its coat clean and shiny. The calf quickly learned to find its way to the cow's udder so that it could have its first drink of the very rich milk.

After calving the cow would produce a lot of milk – too much for her own baby calf and more than enough for our family to use. So my father would pay a visit to Gloucester Cattle Market and purchase two more baby calves. These would arrive home in a cattle lorry and would be put in the cow shed where Dad had put up a special calf pen to keep them warm and comfortable.

In order to make the milk go around we had to hand milk the cow and divide the milk up between the family and the two calves bought at Market. When we had taken as much milk as we needed the newly born calf was allowed to suckle its mother for its feed.

The other two calves were not allowed to suckle the cow because she would not recognise them as her babies and would not allow them to suckle. So we had a lovely job to do and that was to teach the two other calves to drink milk from a bucket. This was not easy at first because the calves were not used to putting their heads into a bucket and just did not know what to do. The knack was to put one hand into the bucket and with our other hand push the calf's head down in the milk. We would then put two or three fingers into its mouth and it would soon get the idea that if it sucked our fingers it was able to drink the milk. Sometimes they would learn quite quickly but occasionally they would take a few days to cotton on to the idea. Once they did it was easy and after a few days they would put their heads in the bucket and drink without the aid of our fingers. When all the milk had been drunk they would get quite cross and start butting the bucket wanting more. After a week or two the cow's own calf was taught to drink from the bucket in the same way.

During the daytime the cow was allowed out into the field to graze on the lush grass which helped produce her milk.

Over the following weeks the calves continued to grow and get quite big. The time came when they were given calf cake to make them strong. They were soon able to go out into the meadow where they would learn to eat grass but they were always ready to come in at milking times to enjoy their bucket of milk. After a few months they would be weaned off milk and would feed on grass and cake and drink water.

Having animals on the smallholding meant that from time to time Dad would have to call the vet if any of the animals were sick or if there was a difficult calving. Our vet was Mr James Murray of Murray Turner and Taylor whose surgery was in The Homend, Ledbury. He was a lovely man and Dad was always pleased to see him.

The calves grew up very quickly and when they were big enough Dad would send them to Market to be sold. I always hoped that the heifer calves would be sold to a dairy farmer where they too could grow into cows and have calves of their own.

DAY-OLD CHICKS

At one time on our smallholding my father kept quite a lot of poultry. In the springtime it was exciting because the day old chicks would be ordered from the hatchery at Newent. About fifty chicks would be ordered and they were delivered in boxes by train to the railway station at Dymock. Each box contained twenty-five tiny chicks.

My father would borrow the tractor from the farm and collect them from the railway station and bring them home. On arrival each box would be checked and the chicks counted.

Then the fun would begin.

The dining room table would be covered with newspaper and we would have some saucers of water and some stale breadcrumbs ready to feed and water the tiny balls of yellow fluff. A box at a time, each chick would be held in the hand and its beak placed into the water, then taken out with its head gently held back and hopefully it would swallow the water. Soon the chicks would get the idea and be able to do it themselves. They would also learn very quickly to peck up the breadcrumbs. The chicks were then put back into their boxes and kept warm by the fire or in the airing cupboard overnight and the same routine would take place the following morning.

Like all children we loved playing with the chicks but soon the time came for them to go into their new home. A big hen house in the The Pleck had been made ready with feeding troughs and water drinkers and most important of all a lovely infra-red lamp was hanging from the roof of the hen house ready for the chicks to huddle under to keep warm.

Occasionally we would have a surprise when some of the older hens would go broody and steal away a nest, usually in the wood pile, hatch their eggs and come back with a clutch of chicks – usually five or six but sometimes as many as ten. If this happened at the same time as the new chicks arrived from the hatchery they would be put together and the mother hen would soon help all the chicks to adapt to their new surroundings. Each day the chicks were fed with a special chick meal and given clean water.

Usually they all thrived but occasionally there would be a disaster and one of the chicks would have been trampled on by the others and died. This would be upsetting for my sister and I and we would find a special place in the garden to bury it. Fortunately this is something which did not happen too often.

The chicks soon grew and changed from balls of fluff to gangly poults with stubby feathers. The chicks that came with the mother hen were quite different from the others. The hatchery chicks were growing up with brown feathers but the intruders were all colours and really stood out from the rest of the chicks.

After several weeks the chicks would be let out into The

Pleck and would run around all day exploring many new nooks and crannies – hiding in the wood pile, chasing the piglets and at times would get out through the wire netting fence and run around chirping getting completely lost. We would have to go and search for them and bring them back safely. Sometimes the cats would help round them up but fortunately did not attempt to catch them in their mouths. Somehow they seemed to know that they were not for them to eat.

Every night at dusk all the chicks and fowls would be driven into their hen houses and be safely shut in for the night in case Mr Fox came hunting. If any had been left out we could be sure that they would go home with him for supper.

Soon these chicks were quite grown up and would be ready to start laying eggs.

And that is another story.

COLLECTING EGGS

Our little chicks soon grew up to become young pullets and were ready for laying eggs.

Each hen house had several nesting boxes at the back which could be inspected by lifting a lid from the outside. These nest boxes would be filled with clean straw and the young pullets would soon learn to go into them to lay their eggs.

The pullets would usually lay one egg a day but sometimes the older hens would lay an extra large egg which usually had two yolks inside instead of one and they were called double yolk eggs.

The eggs were put into a basket or bucket and handled very carefully in order not to crack them. When the hens were disturbed from their nest they would make a lot of cackling noises and go off clucking loudly.

After the eggs had been collected the next job was to wash them and put them into special egg trays each holding two and a half dozen. The trays were then placed into large wooden boxes each holding twelve trays and then they were ready to go to Hawkins egg packing station at nearby Staunton where they would be graded and distributed to the shops.

Hawkins were reluctant to drive their lorry up our narrow sandy lane so Dad would load the large boxes of eggs on to a wheelbarrow and wheel them down to Miss Hart at Stream Cottage at the bottom of the lane where the egg boxes were put into a small barn at the side of her cottage to await collection.

Soon the pullets would have grown into full size hens and then there was another job to be done. We had to put rings on their legs and clip their wings. This job was usually carried out on a Sunday morning and the hens would not be let out as normal. Dad and I would go inside the hen house where the birds would all be sitting on their perches wondering why they had not been let out. One by one I would catch them by their legs and hold them tight while my Dad trimmed a few feathers off one of their wings. This did not hurt them it was just like them having their hair cut. Once this had been done each fowl had a coloured ring put on its leg to identify it from the older hens which already had different coloured rings. The fowls were then let out one at a time into the pleck. I had to make sure the others did not escape when I opened the hen house door. After all had been clipped and ringed they were given their breakfast.

To keep the hens company there were usually two cockerels. These were fine birds and had bright red combs on the top of their heads. Early in the morning these cockerels would wake up and start crowing and were often joined in the chorus by other cockerels from around the village. It was quite a noise but one of the sounds of country life which was accepted by all.

BROODY HENS

There were times when some of our older hens turned broody. My dad told me you could always tell when a hen was broody because she would lose breast feathers and the skin would become very red and warm.

My father would prepare some nest boxes in one of the hen houses and put about twelve eggs on a bed of straw for each broody hen to sit on. The boxes had wooden slats at the front so that the hens could look out but not get out to run around. The hens would sit on the eggs for twenty-one days and every morning and evening they would be let out to have a walk around and eat. They were not usually thirsty because they were provided with water drinkers just outside their nest box and so were able to drink whenever they wished during the day.

Whilst the broody hens were out of their nest boxes, Dad would take the opportunity to check each of the eggs. Each one was held up to his ear and given a shake to see if it was addled meaning that the egg was infertile and would not produce a chick. The hens would return to their nest boxes and they would instinctively turn their eggs and re-arrange them in the straw using their beaks before settling down to continue the incubation.

This process would take three weeks and then there was excitement when the eggs started to hatch. A tiny chip would appear in the egg and we were allowed to hold them and hear the tiny chick inside pecking the shell trying to get out. When the chick had pecked a lot of the shell away it could be seen inside curled up waiting to escape and be free. When they were first hatched they were wet and sticky and not at all like the fluffy new chicks seen on Easter cards.

At times we would help the chick to get out and take away the last bit of shell. As soon as they were able they would run and hide under the wing of the mother hen. The hen would be very proud of her chicks and be very protective. It only took a few hours for the chicks to dry out and turn into tiny balls of yellow fluff. Each time anyone approached the hen house the little chicks would scuttle under the mother hen and cuddle up under her wings.

After a few weeks these hens and chicks would be allowed to roam free in the pleck but each night they would be shut up again to protect them from Mr Fox.

In the late 1950s it became uneconomic to keep poultry on a small scale for egg production and Dad decided to get rid of the poultry apart from a few hens which were kept back to provide eggs for the family.

To utilise the poultry houses a new venture was started with the breeding of domestic rabbits. The rabbits were kept for about eight weeks and then were collected in crates to go to the butchers' shops. My sister Sandra was put in charge of helping with the rabbits and I had very little to do with it.

I have to say that Dad's new venture with the rabbits was short lived.

WASH DAY

Before I started primary school I can remember Monday wash days as being very busy days. Washing would start in the early morning and often last until quite late into the afternoon.

In the lean-to back kitchen there was a large Copper which consisted of a copper cauldron with wooden lid sat in a brick built furnace with a chimney.

The first chore my mother had to do was to carry many buckets of cold water from an outside tap and fill up the copper cauldron. When there was enough water the fire was lit in the furnace and left to heat up the water. In those days our cottage did not have hot and cold running water just cold water from an outside tap. Before the mains water was connected to the cottage we had to rely on water from a well.

In the back kitchen there was a big kitchen table and on it were placed two tin baths and some enamel bowls. These were filled with cold water ready to rinse the clothes when they had been washed.

When the water in the copper was hot enough a little washing soda and grated Sunlight soap would be added and then items which needed to be boiled to get them clean were placed into the copper and the wooden lid put on. Mother often asked my sister or myself to go and check that the copper had not boiled over as this would put out the fire and cause a lot of extra trouble.

The white sheets and pillow cases would be poked and prodded with a stick called a wash dolly until they were clean. The dolly had a long handle and at the end there was an arrangement of three wooden pegs a bit like a small upturned milking stool which was used to stir the washing.

The washing was then transferred to a bowl and put into one of the baths of cold water to be rinsed to get rid of the soap suds. When the rinsing had been completed the final process was to put the washing into a bath of blue water. This water had been treated in a special way. A little blue bag had been squeezed into the cold water turning it blue and after the washing had been rinsed it came out looking sparkling clean and bright and very white. Mother had to be careful not to put too much blue in the water or the effect would be spoilt and the washing would have a blue tint instead of the clean white colour which was desired.

When all the boiling was finished the water was then used to do the hand washing which did not need boiling. This washing was not put into the blue water as it was coloured washing.

Sometimes some of the very dirty washing had to be scrubbed or rubbed up and down on a washboard which consisted of a piece of ribbed metal in a wooden frame. The washing would be rubbed over the ribbed metal which would help get the dirt out. One of Mum's friends in the village had a washboard made of ribbed glass which did the same job.

Clamped to the side of the table was a mangle or wringer which comprised a pair of rollers in a metal frame with a handle. The rinsed washing was passed through the rollers by turning the handle to squeeze as much water out as possible and then all the washing was carried out in wicker baskets to be hung on the washing lines in The Pleck to dry in the sun and wind.

At the end of the afternoon any hot water left in the copper would be used to wash the step inside the front porch. Nothing was wasted.

Ironing was carried out a couple of days later and my sister and I enjoyed helping especially if we could iron the pillow cases and the drying up cloths. Shirts were a bit difficult for us and this was Mum's job. We used heavy flat irons which were heated on the top of the cooking range. To check when they were hot enough we would spit on the flat part of the iron and if it sizzled it was hot enough to use.

Wash Day was a busy and time consuming day and so our main evening meal would usually be cold meat left over from Sunday lunch with mashed potatoes and pickle – I must say I did not like the pickle very much.

LIFE WITHOUT MOD CONS

As a little girl I cannot remember Moors Cottage without mains water but I do remember the old disused well in the front garden. My mother told me that she was always losing teaspoons because my brother would drop them through the gap in the wooden well cover just to hear them plop in the water.

Before mains water was connected Moors Cottage and the other houses in Ryton were reliant on water from our wells. Then one day a new borehole was sunk in the neighbouring village of Bromesberrow Heath which caused many of the wells in the area to go dry including our own well. As a result mains water had to be connected to the affected properties by the Water Company. Our cottage was provided with one outside tap and there were no taps provided inside the cottage.

In the two front rooms of our cottage there were big black fireplaces incorporating ovens called cooking ranges. These kept the cottage warm and heated the kettles to provide hot water.

Bathtime was in a big tin bath in front of the fire. We were always dried and wrapped in a nice warm towel and our clothes were lovely and warm having been warmed on the oven door.

Lighting inside the cottage was from Tilley lamps and candles. At bedtime we would carry a candle up to the bedroom watching the shadows flickering on the walls and ceiling. Mother would usually take the candle back downstairs with her and replace it with a tiny night light standing in a dish of water. This was just in case we ever got frightened in the dark.

Summer nights always seemed to be hot and I can remember going to bed and unable to go to sleep because of the sound of the crickets chirping outside.

In the winter our feather beds were lovely and warm and we had lovely big eiderdowns over the tops of the sheets and blankets. On really cold frosty nights I can remember ice forming on the inside of the window panes and I would make patterns in the ice with my finger.

If we were ever ill in very cold weather and had to stay in bed my mother would light a fire in the small fireplace in the bedroom to keep us warm.

We had no inside toilet but like most cottages we had an outside privy behind the cottage. It was a 'two seater' with a large seat for adults and a smaller seat at a lower level for the children.

Life without mod cons did not seem to us to be out of the ordinary but in 1952 when I was eight years old our lives were about to change – the cottage was going to be modernised. As a family we were to move temporarily to live in the nearby village of Dymock whilst the work was carried out.

That is another chapter.

TIME SPENT IN DYMOCK

In 1952, when I was eight years old, Mr Chew who owned Moors Cottage agreed with my father that the cottage needed renovating and modernising. The whole family had to move out whilst this work was done and we went to live in a red brick house called Stoneberrow Cottages in the centre of Dymock. This was the middle house in a terrace of three and it had steps leading up to the front door. I remember there being a big yellow/brown sink in the kitchen with a draining board and outside in the back yard there was a well with a pump and stone trough.

Living in one of the adjoining houses was an old lady who was a bit of a recluse. We did not see very much of her and I was always a bit frightened of her anyway. It was fun living in the village for the time that we were there. I was able to walk the short distance down the road to Ann Cam Primary School instead of having to catch the school bus from Ryton.

Dymock was a real country village – there was a church, Police House just before the railway bridge, railway station, primary school, two pubs – The Crown and the Beauchamp Arms, two grocery stores one of which had a local bakery at the rear, a post office, butchers shop, Pring's Garage and a local cycle repair shop which I recall also recharged our accumulator batteries which were used in the wireless set we had in the house. It's funny the little things you remember.

The village also had a resident district nurse, Nurse Foster, who visited families in and around the local area and was well known in our village of Ryton.

My best friends in the village were the two sons and elder daughter of the local baker Mr Fawke and they lived in the house opposite. Mr & Mrs Fawke also ran the post office and stores.

This was all very new and interesting and I often paid a visit to the bakery to watch the baker preparing and baking the bread. The bread was sold in their shop and also delivered to many of the villages around Dymock.

The boys were always up to mischief. One day they were over playing at our house when my parents were out. The younger boy Eric was upstairs and he pulled down a bedroom sash window only to get his fingers trapped and we had to call in the postman to help set him free.

On another occasion his elder brother Phillip was in trouble. We were all playing in the back garden and at the top of the garden there were some men digging a big hole, for what reason I cannot recall. We were all sliding down a piece of wood and Phillip fell into the hole dragging an oil can over the top and the contents poured all over him. My mother had to rescue him and I can remember him being sick in the stone pump trough while he was being washed down with cold pump water. Poor kid he was poorly for quite a while.

Once we were playing in their front garden cutting up
pictures we had painted. A pair of scissors was left on the
lawn which I stepped on and they flew up and stuck in the
back of my leg. I rushed home screaming and my mother
and aunt (who was on holiday from London) sat me on the
kitchen draining board trying to stop the flow of blood.
It must have stopped after a while because I am still here
and did not bleed to death as I thought I might have done
at the time.

While we were living in Dymock the cats and other
farm animals were left at Moors Cottage. Each morning
and evening my brother and father would call and feed
them before going to work at The Callow and then would
call again on their way home.

Our pet dog called Sally came to live with us in
Dymock but she would always go to work with Dad and
my brother each morning. She would sit on the cross bar
of my brother's bike with her front paws on the handlebars
and balance all the way to and from Ryton.

At last the renovations were completed and we moved
back into Moors Cottage. We enjoyed our time in Dymock
but it was lovely to return to our cottage to be with all the
animals again.

It was interesting to see what modernisation had taken
place at the cottage whilst we had been away. Part of the
back kitchen had been converted to provide a new bathroom
and toilet and the kitchen had been updated. A new Ideal
range had been fitted in the front living room and this
was fuelled with coal and coke. Outside the chimneys had
been rebuilt, lots of general repairs carried out and a new
septic tank built in the meadow to take the drainage from

the new bathroom and toilet. The other kids in the village were envious and used to say that we were 'posh' because we were one of the few families in the village to have a flush toilet.

Despite all the work on the cottage we still had no electricity but three years later in 1955, when I was eleven, electricity was connected to the cottage. It was a day of great excitement when the electricity was finally switched on. The nicest thing for my mother was having her first electric cooker and washing machine. Oh what a joy to go anywhere in the house and be able to turn on a light with the flick of a switch. No more candles at bedtime.

Incidentally it was some time before Dad allowed us to have our first black and white television but what a treat when we did get one. I remember staying up late to watch the Horse of the Year Show.

Eventually, other cottages and houses in the village were modernised but by no means all of them and many continued to have outside earth closet toilets for several years.

BONNIE, JOLLY AND THE FIELD MARSHALL

When I was very little, before starting primary school, I recall one of my father's workmates Arty Taylor was in charge of the farm's two shire horses called Bonnie and Jolly. Sometimes if the men were working in the fields opposite our cottage Arty would call me over, pick me up and sit me high up on one of the horse's necks behind the big collar. I would then have a lovely ride all the way back to the farm.

When we arrived at the stables the horses were unharnessed, fed and watered and then turned out into the field to run free. This must have been wonderful for them after a long hard working day.

After my father had finished his work for the day at the farm I would have a lift back home sitting on the tiny saddle attached to the crossbar of his bike.

At harvesting time, which was another enjoyable time of the year for the children of the village, we were often to be found in the fields when the binder was reaping the corn. The binder was pulled by one of the shire horses. Great fun was had by all as we raced to help the grownups stack the sheaves of corn into stooks.

Sometimes we were in the fields when the men were taking their tea and if there was a little left over we were often given a cake or some other tit bit. This always tasted nicer than a proper picnic even though it was not a lot of food but just to be able to join with the men was wonderful and we felt so grown up.

After the corn had been reaped we children spent many hours playing hide and seek in and out of the stooks. The only problem playing in the corn stubble was we always went home with scratches up our legs.

A day or so later the sheaves of corn were loaded on to four-wheel wagons and pulled back to the farm by the horses where they were unloaded and put into ricks to await threshing.

After the sheaves had been removed from the field, Mr Chew would allow my dad to put a couple of portable fowl houses in the field so that the hens could glean for the leftover grain which had fallen onto the stubble ground. This meant that on his way to work in the mornings he would have to let the hens out of their houses and in the evening it was my brother's job to ride his bike back to the field to shut the poultry house doors after the hens had gone in to roost. This would hopefully keep them safe from the foxes.

Corn threshing was another exciting time but we were not encouraged to stay too long as it was always very dusty. I suspect this is where my father contracted a disease called Farmers Lung from which he suffered quite badly.

In the late 1940s Mr Chew purchased a new Field Marshall tractor. I recall it was a lovely green colour and in my young mind I considered it to be a great big beast.

I remember watching my dad starting it up and he always made me stand well back. He rolled up some special paper and put it in the end of a metal tube. He then lit the paper and when it was smouldering and glowing he screwed the tube into the engine cylinder at the front of the tractor. In those days Dad smoked his own roll up fags and so he always carried a cigarette lighter in his pocket. He then went round to the side of the tractor and put a long starting handle into the fly wheel and started to swing the handle. This took quite a bit of strength to do but after about three turns the engine fired up and it was all very loud when the engine started. One day the starting handle kicked back towards him as the engine fired and hit his leg causing him quite a lot of injury. Fortunately I was not there on that occasion but I recall he was off work for some time.

I would spend hours sitting on the Field Marshall with Dad ploughing the fields. He would recall how much

My brother, Mike, as a boy standing at the plough behind Bonnie and Jolly in the field opposite Moors Cottage.

easier it was compared with the days when he had to walk all day long behind the plough and shire horses. When my brother was a young boy he would love to go out and watch my dad horse ploughing.

With the advent of the Field Marshall and other tractors, the farm horses became redundant and Bonnie and Jolly were put out to graze.

They had been faithful and hardworking servants and deserved their rest in retirement.

KITTENS

As well as the farm animals on our smallholding we had our own pets. Usually one dog and several cats. The two dogs I remember most of all were Sally and Lassie – they were short haired Jack Russell terriers and were house pets although they were always taken out to work on the farm with my father and brother.

The cats came and went but my sister and I always had one each. These cats sometimes had kittens which caused great excitement. They slept in the sheds with the dogs amongst the bales of hay and straw. Occasionally one cat would appear on the doorstep of the porch carrying a kitten in her mouth, drop it on the doormat and go off again to the shed only to reappear a few minutes later with another kitten. She would do this several times and end up with three or four kittens on the doorstep.

My mum, sister and I would find a large cardboard box, fill it with straw and an old jumper and put the kittens into it. They would soon be joined by the mother cat. These kittens were so tiny and would be blind with their eyes tightly closed until about ten days when their eyes would open. Soon these little ones would start exploring and as they grew up they would be taken with the box and mother cat back to the shed to sleep.

My sister and I would spend many hours with them in the sheds but were always told not to mess with them too much or the mother cat would leave them.

The cat was very proud of her kittens but was very good and let us pick them up and hold them. They were lovely little things and brought us much pleasure.

We even tucked them up in a dolls pram and took them for walks down the lane and we were upset if they ever jumped out and ran back to mother.

I think it was a good job we were at school most of the day or the kittens would have been loved to death!

ORPHAN LAMBS

In the early spring when it was lambing time at The Callow my father would sometimes arrive home from work with two or three baby lambs. Occasionally a ewe would give birth to triplets and could only feed two of them. This meant that one of them might have to be bottle fed. Also sadly a ewe might die leaving orphan lambs which again had to be bottle fed. Farmers referred to these as tiddlers.

Mr Chew would sometimes give Dad a few of these lambs to take back to the cottage to be fed and looked after.

These little lambs were made cosy in one of the sheds in a pen made up of straw bales and would be fed with cow's milk from a bottle. On the top of the bottle was attached a special rubber lamb teat which Dad usually purchased from the local chemist. The lambs would soon learn to suck the teat and drink and enjoy the warm milk. They were fed every couple of hours to begin with so this was a full time job for my mother. Needless to say when my sister and I were home from school there was never any trouble getting us to go and feed the lambs. It was great fun and when the lambs had finished the milk they butted the bottle to see if there was any milk left.

The lambs soon started to grow and after a couple of weeks they were able to go out into the meadow. At feeding times we would go out and call them and they would come running up to the wire fence and we would push the bottles through the wire netting and they would have their drink before running off to continue playing.

Sometimes when we girls were out playing they would come up to the fence thinking it was feeding time. When the lambs were small we were allowed to have them on the lawn to play with and sometimes we would take them for a walk along the lane. This was fun as they were quite tame and attached to us almost as if we were their mothers. They seldom made any attempt to run away.

As they grew older they would be fed with meal and lamb pellets out of a trough and would gradually be weaned off the milk. They would often share in the same trough as the pigs which was an amusing sight.

As time went on the lambs grew and grew and were eventually big enough to be sold at market. I must say it was a sad day when we had to say goodbye to them but somehow we always knew we would have some new baby lambs the following spring.

PIGS AND PIGLETS AND A TRIP TO THE BOAR

Some way down the path from the cottage there was a small collection of farm buildings made up of fodder sheds, cattle loose houses and brick pig sties. In the pig sties at different times of the year there were pigs of all ages –sows with litters of young piglets, expectant sows, gilts (young female pigs who have not had their first litter), weaners (young pigs no longer reliant on their mother's milk and able to feed on meal and water) and pigs fattening ready to go to market.

When the female pigs came into season – or as Dad used to say start pigging – we would have to take them to the boar. Dad did not have a boar on our smallholding and so he would take his sows, one at a time, to a neighbouring farmer's boar to be served.

This entailed a two mile walk to Mr Harry Shayle's farm at nearby Ketford. It would usually take two or three people to walk the sow to the farm and my sister, brother and I often helped. We girls were sent ahead to make sure all the cottage and field gates were shut and my brother and my dad would take up the rear and drive the sow along the way. Although it was a long walk it did not take too long to get to Little Ketford Farm because the sow would usually trot along the road rather than saunter – she knew where she was going!

On arrival at Mr Shayle's farm the sow would be introduced to the boar and would then be left for a couple of days for the business to be done. It was then a matter of us all setting off on foot back to Ketford and walking the sow back home. For some reason she never seemed to be in quite so much hurry to go home!

Sows have a gestation period of three months, three weeks and three days. When they were near to farrowing they would make a nest in the pig sty with extra straw. Usually they gave birth (farrowed) during the night time but occasionally they would give birth during the daytime and then we were allowed to stand very quietly and watch as the baby piglets arrived into the world. These tiny pink piglets could soon stand up and walk and would very quickly learn where to find a teat to suckle on their mother's belly. Each piglet would have its own teat and would struggle to get to it scrambling over one another to do so.

When piglets are not feeding they sleep for long periods and my father would put an infra-red pig lamp for the tiny babies to sleep under well out of the way of their mother who sometimes through her clumsy way would tend to lie on her piglets if they were not quick enough to get out of the way. This would also enable the mother pig to go out to feed and walk around the pleck while the little ones were kept snug and warm under the lamp in the sty.

Occasionally one of the piglets would be much smaller than the rest of the litter and this would be called the runt.

Very often this tiny piglet would not be strong enough to find a teat to suckle so it would be taken up to the house, put into a box of straw, and kept warm in front of the oven range which was continually alight all day and night, summer and winter. The little pig would be given warm cow's milk and when it was strong enough it was taken back to suckle from its mother. The runt piglets never grew as fast and big as the other piglets and so they tended to become pets and when all the other piglets went to market this one stayed behind to grow up at home.

Soon the piglets would be strong enough to go out into the meadow with their mother and would have a wonderful time exploring their new surroundings. If two sows farrowed at the same time it was important to keep their piglets apart for a few weeks so as not to get them mixed up – but no doubt they all knew which was their real mother.

The sows would rout about all day long and at times would lie down in the grass to feed their young – a really lovely sight. After the piglets had been fed they would go one at a time to the mother pig's head and kiss her nose as if to say 'thank you'.

They would soon grow and be able to feed out of a trough eating special pig meal and drinking water. They were then known as weaners because they had been weaned off their mother's milk. At eight to ten weeks Dad would usually take the weaners off to market to be sold on to other farmers to fatten into pigs for pork and bacon. Sometimes the buyers might keep some of the young female pigs to breed and have little ones of their own.

HELPING IN THE FIELDS

I had many friends in Ryton and one of my best friends, Wendy, lived on the other side of the village with her parents Gard and Marge Powell and her many brothers and sisters at Lime Tree Villa where they had a small farm growing strawberries, raspberries, apples and cherries. The village kids were allowed to earn pocket money picking these fruits to go to market.

Picking fruit was not such good fun as our job of minding the cherries on the trees. We were not paid for this but in the evenings after school I would go up into the village and help Wendy and the other Powell kids keep the starlings off the cherry trees. Starlings were greedy birds and would pinch many cherries given half a chance. We would have long sticks which we would hit against pieces of tin hanging from the branches. This would make a terrible noise and certainly scared the birds. I really wonder who ate most cherries the kids or the starlings!

During the summer it was especially busy on our smallholding because it was hay-making time.

This was hard work and had to be completed in good time before rain came to spoil the hay. All the equipment needed for hay-making was borrowed from The Callow where my father worked. Once the hay had been mowed and turned to dry in the wind and sun it was time for it to be baled. Dad would drive the tractor with the baler and my brother Mike would pass the bales up to me on the trailer and I would stack them to the best of my ability ready for transporting to a large timber barn next to Stream Barn Cottage just below our cottage. This was great fun but hard work.

Harvest time was also another highlight of the year on The Callow. During late July and early August the fields of corn were ripe and ready for harvesting. I remember when the horse drawn binder and reaper was replaced by a new combine harvester. This made harvesting much easier and less labour intensive. Mrs Chew or sometimes my mother would take tea out to the farmworkers and if we children were lucky enough to be in the fields at that time we were usually given a small tit bit. This tea was very welcome for the men because they would be working until dark and it would be many hours before they could get home for their evening meal.

If the corn fields were close to our cottage we would congregate with other children and older boys from the village. We would stand spaced out around the edge of the field hoping to see a fox run out or the older boys hoping to let the dogs loose to catch a rabbit for a meal next day. We would stay until the last square of corn was cut because quite often the fox would hide in the standing corn until the very last minute when it would make a break and run for its life. At the end of the day the kids would walk home along the lanes singing, tell stories or more likely arguing over some trivial matter.

When all the corn had been harvested the baler would go into the fields to bale up the straw which was taken to be stored in the barns back at the farm ready for bedding down the cattle in the winter.

When the mangolds and sugarbeet were ready for harvesting, the men would go out into the fields to pull the roots, and then Mum and a few of the local women would cut the tops off with a special root knife and stack the roots in tumps. This work was very hard and often wet and cold.

The mangolds would be carted back to a field near the farm where they would be stored in large tumps covered with straw and earth and then used later in the winter for feeding the cattle. The sugarbeet would be loaded on to trailers and taken to the railway station at Dymock, loaded on to goods wagons and taken by train to the sugarbeet factory at Kidderminster.

Throughout the year there was other work to be done at home such as cleaning out the animals and during the winter months transporting hay bales up from Stream Barn to our cattle sheds.

When the snow came that was another game. One winter there was so much snow our high sided lane was filled and we could walk over the top of the hedges into the fields. There was also so much frost which went on for several weeks and eventually the water pipes froze under the ground. There was one pipe down in the village which was not frozen and I can remember walking all day carrying buckets of water for the animals. This went on for several days until the thaw eventually came.

Helping Dad on the holding and being with the farm workers in the fields was all part of growing up in the country and something I would not have missed for the world.

PLAYTIMES AND MINDING THE COWS

I mentioned earlier that my friend Wendy and her family lived on a small fruit farm on the other side of the village which had many barns and outbuildings. Some weekends all the boys and girls from the village would congregate there for a game of hide and seek. It was great fun as there were so many places to hide – in the hay bales, in the pig sties, in the hen houses and in the meal sheds. Hours and hours were spent just playing around the farm yard.

Some of the girls had a den in an old shed where there was an old table, an old broken chair, straw bales and empty oil cans turned upside down. We would spend many happy hours playing and having picnics.

The woods in Ryton were also a great playground for we kids and often we would go off for the whole day walking and playing in the woods, occasionally ending up at the neighbouring village of Ketford where the River Leadon ran under a large stone bridge. I think in latter years there was also another reason to go there as some of the boys living in Ketford were an attraction to some of the girls from Ryton.

My sister, Sandra, and I were also friendly with two

boys Martin and Tim Vernall who lived at Field Cottage just across the field from our home. They lived there with their parents and grandparents. In their garden they had an apple tree and in our garden we had a big plum tree. These two trees were used as vantage points. If they got up into their apple tree and I climbed up into our plum tree we could shout to one another. After lunchtimes in the summer school holidays we would each wait for a signal that all was clear for us to go out and play again.

We spent many hours playing with Martin and Tim and sometimes we were joined by some of their cousins who would travel from Ledbury to visit their grandparents and the family. They would catch the train to Dymock and from there walk out to Ryton. These cousins were all boys and my sister and I were outnumbered usually by four boys to two girls.

Picnics would be packed and off we would go for the day just walking the fields and making our way towards the River Leadon. We were always very sensible and never got too near the water as we had been warned of the whirlpools that could suck you under if you fell in.

In the summer evenings after school I would pass away many an hour sat up on the roofs of Dad's sheds and pig cots. I would sit there just singing or shouting to my heart's content or even just sitting quietly watching the hens and pigs running around the pleck.

At the bottom of Sandy Lane where it joined the Dymock to Ryton road there was a tiny ford with a small concrete footbridge on one side of it. The water from the stream did not flow over the ford very often – only during the winter months. I would spend the odd half hour sat there while my mother chatted with one of her neighbours Lil Millard. As a young girl I can also remember playing for hours in the sand in the lane – no traffic to worry about in those days.

In the autumn when the plums were ripe I would sit up in the tree eating them. They were a variety called Dymock and were delicious dessert plums which could be eaten without cooking. I was often told by my mother I would end up with tummy ache but I can't remember suffering too much from that.

There was a stream which ran from Quabbs Wood along the edge of the fields towards Quabbs Cottage. Consequently some of these fields were boggy with lots of grassy tufts in them which were great fun to play in. One of our favourite games was 'feet off the ground' where we would stand on these little grassy hillocks jumping from one to another and trying not to get caught out.

Towards the bottom of the lane there was a meadow used by the local lads as a football pitch. Every Saturday there would be a match between the locals and lads from some of the surrounding villages. Quite often my brother would play and I would go down and stand on the touch line to watch. Some years later my brother developed cartilage trouble in his knee and had to have an operation. He always said it was the result of playing football on rough ground.

Some of my friends lived at the bottom of the little back lane at a smallholding called Quabbs Cottage. Here lived the Shayle family and they kept house cows and sent their milk to the Milk Factory.

After school each day in the summer months two of

their girls, Dinah and Iris, were expected to take the cows out of the fields and lead them along the lanes to graze. We called this Minding the Cows. Sometimes I would go along to have someone to play with and quite often we would be joined by other kids from the village. The cows would come up the back lane behind our cottage and out along Sandy Lane as far as the lane leading to The Hill Farm. The cows would meander along grazing the verges whilst we played together. I always had to make sure that our back garden gate was closed to prevent the cows straying into our garden

Frequently there were squabbles amongst the kids so when this happened we went home early leaving the Shayle girls on their own to make their way back home with the cows.

My Dad's boss Mr Chew had a lovely herd of pedigree Hereford Cattle. One spring day I remember my father and some of the other farm hands from The Callow were moving the Hereford cows and their calves to Mr Chew's off-lying farm buildings and cattle yard at Limetrees on the other side of Ryton. This meant walking the cattle through the middle of the village where there were lots of kids, including me, playing near The Green and telephone box. The men shouted to us get out of sight. Unfortunately I did not run as fast as the others and one of the cows spotted me. She chased after me and it was only luck that I managed to jump over an iron garden gate leading into Limetrees House before she managed to set about me. My father was quite worried at the time because cows with calves can be very protective and dangerous. Luckily all was well but we were always warned after that to stay out of fields if the cows had their calves with them. We were told they could be just as dangerous as a bull.

At the top of the meadow below our cottage there were some big trees and two of them had branches reaching to the ground. We kids would sit on these branches with our feet on the ground and use them as a see-saw. We could also climb up into the middle of the trees and get lost among the branches. Sadly this meadow with its trees along with the ford and its footbridge disappeared when the M50 motorway was built.

WILD DAFFODILS

When I was growing up as a young girl in Ryton in the 1950s there were many old pasture meadows around the village. At the bottom of Sandy Lane the fields next to Stream Cottage were known as the Water Meadows and the two fields running alongside the road to Dymock opposite Field Cottage were known as the The Moors and The Castles. A stream which started as a spring in Quabbs Wood ran down past Quabbs Cottage, through a little ford with a footbridge, then continued meandering its

way to another ford at the bottom of our lane near Stream
Cottage and on through the meadows towards the Callow
Farm. Frequently in wet winter months the stream would
burst its banks and the meadows below us would flood –
hence their name the Water Meadows.

When winter had passed and spring arrived the
meadows were transformed into carpets of yellow wild
daffodils which lasted from mid-March to early April.

The surrounding woods and countryside were ablaze
with these dainty spring flowers which stretched to the
neighbouring villages of Dymock, Kempley, Oxenhall,
Bromesberrow, Ketford and Redmarley.

Since my childhood days so many of the meadow habitats
have disappeared, mainly due to modern agricultural
practices and many were lost when the motorway was built.

My father told me that before I was born there used
to be special day trips on trains from London to Newent
and Dymock railway stations called the 'Daffodil Specials'
when people would come to see the daffodils and to pick
them. Between the two Wars the picking and selling of
wild daffodils provided an extra means of income for
the local people and was an important part of the local
economy. By the time I was born those railway excursions
had finished.

However when I was a girl the picking of daffodils was
customary and the wild daffodils were picked by local
people, including school children, and sent to London by
train to be sold at the major flower markets in London and
The Midlands and other destinations.

Many of the ladies and especially the teenage girls in
the village spent days in the fields and woods picking

and bunching up the flowers and even we children went picking in the evenings after school. We would earn quite a lot of pocket money doing this and it was a time of the year much enjoyed by us all.

A lady in our village, Mrs Ivy Davies, lived close by in a cottage known as No 333 Ryton and she had a collection point at her cottage where local people would deliver the bunches of daffodils they had picked. She would pack them into boxes and send them off to Dymock railway station bound for London and other parts of the country. I remember helping her to pack the boxes and I enjoyed seeing the many addresses to where they were to be dispatched. She told me that the customers would send her postal orders in advance to pay for the flowers and the transport. Many of the flowers went to Hospitals and churches, especially at Easter time.

Looking back, the wild daffodils were so much a part of my childhood but thankfully they are now protected and no longer picked.

SCHOOL DAYS

Most of the kids from the Ryton area went to Ann Cam Primary School in Dymock and this is the school I attended as did my sister and our elder brother.

Sandra and I along with other children from our side of the village would meet the bus at the bottom of Sandy Lane and it would go on towards Ryton via The Rocks to pick up children from the Ketford road. Then into the village where more children would be waiting by the telephone box on the Green. The bus then went on to Dymock via Bromesberrow Heath, Brooms Green and Greenway collecting more school kids on the way.

When the school bus left Bromesberrow Heath it took a short cut down the narrow lane which led to Haffield and Brooms Green. In a cottage at the end of

Sandra and Christine at
Ann Cam Primary School

this lane on the left hand side lived an old lady whom the kids nicknamed Shooky Brookes. Whenever the bus passed her cottage she would run out of her gate waving her arms and shaking her broom at the driver and all the kids would stand up cheering and waving their arms which annoyed her even more.

A few local children went to a very tiny school at Haffield which was on the road between Bromesberrow Heath and Brooms Green. This little school eventually closed down in the early 1950s when there were only about twelve children attending and they then went to the primary school at Dymock.

Ann Cam School had five classes when I was there, with about 20–25 pupils in each class. It was on the whole a very friendly school but one girl I remember who came from just outside Dymock was the school bully and most of the kids were frightened of her. She quite often picked on me and bullied me a lot. This would go on for a while until she got tired of picking on me and set on someone else. It was not a nice experience and I would often get upset and not want to go to school. I don't think I ever told my mum because that was not the done thing in those days.

The children in classes one and two sat together in the school hall each with its own teacher. It was not always easy to concentrate because we were often distracted by the other class.

During the mid morning break we were all given a small bottle of milk to drink. These bottles contained 1 gill which was a liquid measure of about a quarter of a pint. I absolutely hated milk – it made me feel sick and I refused to drink it. I would be kept in class during playtime with this bottle of milk with a straw pushed through the middle of the cardboard top. I would take a sip now and again but could never finish it before lessons started again. So the teacher would put the bottle to one side and I would be presented with it again at playtime in the afternoon. By this time it had started to smell and I always hoped it had gone off so that I would not have to drink it. After a few months my mother wrote a letter to the school to say that I could not drink milk and asked that it should not be given to me. What a relief that was. It might sound strange that despite living on a smallholding with our own house cow I could not drink milk.

When I started Secondary School I used to have to help out at home after returning from school by hand milking the cow. I had no problem doing the milking but I would leave it to the calves and the rest of the family to drink the milk!

Back at Primary School the cardboard milk bottle tops were saved to be used to make fluffy woollen pom-poms. Two cardboard tops were put together and coloured wool was wrapped around the edges and through the hole in the middle and this continued until the hole was full of wool. Then the wool was cut around the edges with scissors and a piece of wool was placed between the two cardboard tops and tied tight. The cardboard was removed to leave a lovely fluffy pom pom.

Class three was much better. It was a smaller class with few distractions apart from looking through the window seeing the other children playing games in the back school yard.

During break times we always played games in the

playground. Skipping was very popular especially 'All in together Girls', where two girls held the ends of a long rope and swung it whilst the other girls ran in and started skipping to the chant:

All in together girls – this fine weather girls
When it is your birthday please run out

We would all then chant the months of the year to the rhythmn of the skipping rope.

There were several ball games and running games played by the boys and the girls. Tag was always a favourite and to decide who was going to be the chaser one of the group would go round in a circle tapping the other kids chanting:

Ibble obble black bobble
Ibble obble out.

The first three classes in the school were taught by lady teachers but in class four we were taught by a man, Mr Jenkins who lived in a house opposite the school. He was quite a character and would often throw rubbers at the boys if they were not paying attention. Sometimes he would walk around the classroom and if you were not doing something right he would tap you on the head with a big book. This was not funny and it would hurt quite a lot. I was quite happy in this class but when I was older I was much happier in the top class five.

In this class we were taught by the headmaster Mr Jack Hobbs who lived on the outskirts of the village near the Cricket Ground. It was the duty of one of the boys in this class to mix up the school ink. This was blue/black powder mixed with water – often quite a messy job. Also one of the boys had the duty of ringing the school bell to let everyone know when to change classes or stop for playtime or dinner time. This bell was quite big and was hung high up on the outside wall of the top classroom. The bell was rung using a long rope attached to the clanger.

I remember when I was in my final year at primary school we had a very hard winter and one morning I woke quite poorly. I couldn't lift my head off the pillow and couldn't stand bright light. The doctor was called and he arranged for an ambulance to take me to Over Isolation Hospital, near Gloucester with suspected meningitis. After four days in an isolation room I recovered and much to the relief of my parents I was allowed home. It was thought that my condition was as a result of playing outside in the snow in extremely cold weather. The following week I was back in the classroom.

Our school had a wonderful kitchen and the school cooks prepared lunch for all the pupils and staff. It was always freshly cooked and I remember the meals were delicious. In order that the meal room could cope with all the pupils there were two sittings. While the children on the first sitting were eating, the others were outside playing; then we all swapped over.

The school did not have inside flush toilets. The girls' toilets were outside in the corner of the playground. They were always cold and wet and not very pleasant to use at the best of times. The washhand basins were in another part of the school building and there was only a cold tap to wash your hands.

The vicar of Dymock, Revd Gethyn-Jones, came to the Primary School every Friday and sometimes he took the senior children back to the church for R.E. lessons. Occasionally he would take us up the church tower so that we could look out over the village from very high up.

The school children always took produce and flowers to decorate the church porch for Harvest Festivals and we would have a special children's Harvest Service in the afternoon before the main Harvest Festival in the evening.

After two years in the top class we were ready to sit our eleven plus exam and get ready to move on to secondary school. Unfortunately I did not pass my exam and at the beginning of the next autumn term I started at Newent Secondary Modern School. The kids that did pass the exam went to the Grammar School in Newent.

To get to the Newent schools we travelled on the same school bus as the primary school children.

The young children were dropped off in Dymock and we older ones travelled on to Newent collecting the older Dymock children who had been waiting on the village green. When the River Leadon was in flood, as it often did in the winter, it would be great fun for we school kids if the bus arrived at the river and found that it had risen too high for even the bus to get through. The bus had to turn around and drop off all the kids to go home and we missed a day at school.

The secondary school was on two sites and we often went from one site to the other for different lessons. The school playing field was quite a long walk from the school buildings on the main road leading out of Newent towards Dymock. Games days were great fun but I often wonder where we got the energy to play games after such a long walk from the school and then back after an afternoon sports. We always made it – plenty of exercise in those days.

My days at senior school were very enjoyable and it was a sad day when I left in the summer of 1960 to start my first job in Ledbury as a junior receptionist at C. T. & G. H. Smith the auctioneers.

THE BUILDING OF THE M50 MOTORWAY

In the spring of 1958 something happened which was to change our village and the surrounding district for ever – construction started on the new M50 motorway. It was one of the first motorways to be built in Britain and it was to start from a new bypass being constructed around the market town of Ross-on-Wye and would end near Tewkesbury. We were told it would also be known as the Ross Spur Motorway.

When news first reached us that a motorway was to be built it was quite a bone of contention in the area but once things got under way it was a most interesting time for all the people living in the village watching day by day and month by month as things changed and began to take shape.

The route of the motorway would cut through Ryton and would separate our cottage and our immediate neighbours from the rest of the village. However there was to be a new bridge over the motorway at the bottom of our lane so we would not be permanently cut off. The motorway was only a few hundred yards from our cottage and when the section through our village was being built we could look down on it and watch everything happening.

Many things which were so familiar to us were lost. The little stone footbridge by the ford at the bottom of Sandy Lane, where we sat as kids, soon disappeared as did the tiny stream which was diverted into large drains and culverts. The lovely water meadows also disappeared under tarmac. Once the new bridge had been completed the Dymock road and Sandy Lane were once again linked to our village of Ryton and the village of Bromesberrow Heath.

Whilst construction was taking place I remember our school bus had to be diverted in many directions over many months.

Two young lads who worked for the road contractors Douglas Construction stayed at our cottage as lodgers whilst they were working in the area. They were very pleasant and polite and worked very long hours including lots of weekends. My mother enjoyed having them with us and the extra income was very welcome. This was an extremely busy time for her – cooking, washing, keeping the house in order as well as her outside work on the land.

Eventually work was completed and at the end of 1960 the motorway was opened. It was very strange looking down from our cottage and seeing cars and lorries whizzing by at high speed through our previously peaceful countryside. When one of our neighbours drove us along the motorway for the first time it was quite a thrill and interesting to see how much it had changed the surrounding landscape and villages around the area. As we drove along we tried to spot local places and landmarks from new unfamiliar angles. Now after so many years it would be hard to remember how the landscape looked before the construction work had begun. The M50 is still considered to be one of the most attractive motorways ever built.

Our newspapers were delivered by the local milkman. As we were self sufficient with our own house cow we did not need a delivery of milk, and so he left our papers in a drain pipe tied to the fence near the motorway bridge. When my sister and I were not at school we would take it in turns to walk down the lane with the dog to collect the papers. It always took much longer than it did before the motorway was built because we would stand on the new bridge watching the traffic passing by and wondering where it was all coming from and going to.

A section of the M50 between Ryton and Ross-on-Wye was constructed through the middle of Dymock Wood – a beautiful wood which was, and still is, famous for its wild daffodils. The lads who stayed with us told us that when the route of the motorway was excavated through the woods, the top soil was put to one side and when the road had been completed this top soil was spread on the side embankments. When the first spring arrived after the opening of the motorway swathes of daffodils appeared where the top soil had been spread.

One amusing story we heard was that because the M50 was one of the first motorways to be built many of the motoring public were unaware of the restrictions on its use. So when the daffodils appeared some motorists stopped to pick them and on one occasion a party of motorists was seen parked on the hard shoulder with a picnic table set up.

A couple of years after the motorway had been completed it was extended at the Tewkesbury end to link up with the newly built M5.

Before and after. The picture at the top shows two young girls playing in the ford at the bottom of Sandy Lane with a horse and corn drill from Callow Farm heading off to the fields. This ford and the stream which meandered through the watermeadows is now part of the southbound carriageway of the M50 motorway. The colour picture shows wild daffodils growing on the roadside verge near Sandy lane. The motorway bridge leading to Ryton is built over where the ford used to be.

DYMOCK RAILWAY STATION ON THE GLOUCESTER TO LEDBURY BRANCH LINE

About two miles from our home at Ryton we had a wonderful facility – the railway station at Dymock. The station was on the Ledbury to Gloucester line and was very busy in those days. Our family used it quite a lot – mainly on Saturdays when my mum and Dad along with my sister Sandra and I would ride our bikes to catch the train to Gloucester. This was always a special treat which we looked forward to very much.

From Dymock the train passed through Newent station and several country halts. Shortly after leaving Dymock we would arrive at Four Oaks Halt and then on to Newent Station. Continuing on our journey we would pass through Malswick Halt, Barbers Bridge Station and then on to Gloucester. Here, passengers who wanted to travel further afield could catch trains to London Paddington and South Wales.

I remember Dymock Station having lovely colourful flower borders and it was always beautifully kept by the station staff. The signalman was a local lady, Gladys Badham, and I think she was the only lady signalman on the line.

Sometimes we would take the train to Ledbury and we would pass through Greenway Halt and then Ledbury Halt, on the outskirts of the town, before the final short journey to the main railway station in Ledbury. I would frequently ride my bike down to Greenway and catch the train to Ledbury. This little Halt comprised a small ash platform with a wooden shelter and was set in a cutting reached by a path from the road.

Dymock always had a very busy goods yard and before I was born large quantities of timber would be transported to many destinations including pit props to the coal pits in South Wales.

When I was a girl there would be livestock wagons which would take the stock to Market. Gloucester Station was close to the Cattle Market and the stock would be walked from the train to the market.

Sugar Beet was an important crop in our district and the local farmers would take the harvested sugar beet to the station where it would be loaded on to the goods wagons and transported to the Sugar Beet factory at Kidderminster to be refined. Dad's boss Mr Chew grew sugar beet on The Callow and each year Dad and some of the other farm workers would haul loads of beet to Dymock Station.

I have heard my father speak of the days when trainloads of fruit and hop pickers from as far afield as Kent would be brought to Dymock and other stations and halts along the line for seasonal work and as I mentioned in an earlier chapter many day trippers would travel on the famous 'Daffodil Specials' to see and pick the wild daffodils.

In my early years the trains were pulled by steam locomotives and as a little girl I remember them being very

Dymock station in the late 1950s. The gardens on both platforms were always colourful and well tended.

Taken by Dennis Norton in September 1963, four years after the station was closed for passenger traffic. How sad to see this lovely station looking so desolate and what a loss to the local community. The goods shed and signal box can be seen in the distance. The line to Gloucester remained open for freight traffic until 1964. (D. J. Norton Collection)

noisy, billowing smoke and steam. I loved the sound of their whistles and the chuff-chuff-chuff as they pulled out of the station. When I grew older the steam trains were replaced by smaller diesel trains but they did not have the character of the steam locomotives.

The railway connections were so important to the people in our rural areas but sadly it all came to an end in 1959 when the Branch Line was closed to passenger traffic. It was such a disappointment to rural folk for whom the railways were a life line.

The section of line between Dymock and Gloucester continued to be used for goods traffic but the line from Dymock to Ledbury was closed for all traffic. Then in 1964, following the Beeching Report which recommended closing down hundreds of branch lines all over the country, the line between Dymock and Gloucester was closed completely.

Now the stations and the branch line had all gone. What a sad time that was.

TO MARKET

To market, to market to buy a fat pig
Home again, home again jiggety jig

Whenever I was on holiday from school and a trip to Gloucester Cattle Market was in the offing I would always be pleading with my father to let me go with him. Maybe it was to sell weaners or a sow with her litter or perhaps buy some calves. Whatever, I was always keen to go.

The morning of market day was an early start. Up with the lark dressed and ready, waiting for the haulage lorry to arrive. Dad always used Gouldings Transport from Newent and I got to know their drivers well. Sometimes we would be the first pick-up of the morning but on occasions there would already be stock on the lorry. The pigs or whatever stock was going to market would be loaded on to the lorry and partitioned from any other stock with gates inside the lorry. They might sometimes have to go up a ramp to the upper deck of the lorry. This was not quite as easy as the animals were not used to going up ramps into confined spaces but with a lot of shouting and shooing the driver in the end got them to go where he wanted them.

When all was loaded together with a bale of straw for bedding the animals down in the market pens, off we would go to Gloucester Market.

Although this day was exciting it was also sad seeing the animals leaving their home environment.

In those days my father did not have a car and so we would hitch a lift in the lorry.

The lorry driver usually had more farms to call at to make collections before we eventually arrived at the market. This journey could easily take a couple of hours. One exciting part of the trip was if the driver stopped *en route* at a bakers shop to buy cream cakes or doughnuts – one for Dad, one for me and one for himself – this was a real treat.

On arrival at the market the stock was unloaded at different sections depending what animals were on board. Dad usually took pigs to market and these were unloaded in the Pig Section and allocated a specific pen number. Before they went into the pen, the straw which had been brought from home was scattered in the pen to make the animals comfortable and keep them clean and presentable for sale.

I was quite a tiny tot but loved the atmosphere in the market and all the chit-chat that went on prior to the auction. Dad would know a lot of the farmers and dealers and had a good day out catching up on all the news and gossip.

I was fascinated listening to the auctioneer talking so loud and fast. Sometimes the animals did not reach the price the farmer wanted and the farmers and dealers could then be seen haggling and trying to do a private deal with each other. Eventually after much argument they would come to an agreement on price. Each would then spit on the palm of his hand then shake hands to show the deal had been done. Dad told me this was the custom.

When our own stock had been sold, Dad would sometimes buy some replacement pigs or calves or even a few young store cattle. This meant a return ride in the cattle lorry. If on the other hand no purchases were made it was a trip home on the bus from Gloucester Bus Station to Dymock. Quite an experience round the country lanes visiting villages on the way. On arrival in Dymock it then meant a two-mile walk back to the cottage. I always hoped Dad would buy some animals in the market so that we could ride home in the lorry saving a long tiring walk at the end of a busy day.

When I was in my early teens, Dad treated himself to a Vespa motor scooter which completely transformed his life. He was now able to get to Gloucester and Ledbury Markets under his own steam which made life so much easier for him.

After leaving school aged fifteen I started my first job in Ledbury. At times when I was not riding my bike into Ledbury I would catch the bus at Greenway Cross with some of the other girls from my village. Sometimes whilst we were waiting for the bus on Market Days a Gouldings cattle lorry would pass by and the driver would stop to give us a lift. The drivers had worked with their firm for many years and they had seen many of us girls grow up through our school years and into our teens. They certainly remembered me from my trips with Dad to Gloucester Market.

My first job was with C. T. & G. H. Smith, the auctioneers in Ledbury who ran Ledbury Cattle Market. Luckily I already knew quite a lot about markets from my visits with Dad but now I was going to market to work.

It was here I met Jim, my husband to be, and so ended up marrying a livestock auctioneer. Dad was very pleased because when we were courting he used to enjoy talking to Jim about the animals and markets and they had a lot in common.

SLAUGHTERING THE PIG

I must warn readers that they may find my next childhood memory rather gruesome but what I am about to recall was very much part of country life when I was a little girl. It was a time when smallholders had to be self sufficient with food, particularly during the years of rationing following the War. I remember it being said that a weekly food ration of bacon and ham was just four ounces per adult. How fortunate we were having our own smallholding with a plentiful supply of pig meat and bacon for our own consumption.

My dad always reared pigs and there was always one pig that would be kept and fattened to provide food for the family. When this pig had reached a good weight the time would come for it to be slaughtered.

Some friends of my parents were a German couple, Hans and Margaret, who lived in one of the neighbouring villages. Hans had been a prisoner of war and had stayed in this country after the war had ended. Hans worked on one of the local farms but was also a qualified slaughterman and was called upon by many butchers, farmers and smallholders to carry out the slaughter of their animals.

It was a sad day when the time came for the slaughter of the pig. I remember it quite vividly.

A bed of straw would be made in the pleck or back garden and the pig would be led up from the shed or pig sty with a rope tied over the upper part of its snout. The pig would be grunting and squealing and making a terrible din. I would be scared stiff and would run upstairs and put my head under some pillows and hold them tight over my ears until I could not hear any more squealing. I knew then that it was OK to go out and see the rest of the activities.

The pig had been humanely shot and bled and was now lying on the bed of straw. The straw was then lit and a good fire was encouraged to burn in order to singe off all the bristles on the pig's skin. After all the bristles had been singed the washing and scraping would take place. I shall always remember the smell of the straw and bristles burning.

After this had been done the washing and scraping would take place. Scraping was done with a large knife and scrubbing brush and many buckets of water to rinse off the singed bristles.

Sometimes I would be brave enough to help scrape off the bristles but it was always with a little bit of sadness that I did this – poor old pig.

Once the pig was clean it would be hung up by its back legs on a ladder and placed against the back wall of the cottage. The slaughterman would then set about his next task. The chitterlings and innards of the pig had to be removed. This was a skilled job and done carefully. The chitterlings would be put into a bath and one of our neighbours, Mr Taylor, from Stream Barn Cottage would collect them and take them home to wash them very thoroughly and use them to prepare brawn. He would also take the trotters to use.

One thing which was not given away, as it was used by my mother to make faggots, was the veil. This looked like a lace veil and was made up of transparent membrane and bits of lard scattered within it.

After these formalities had been carried out the pig would be carried on the ladder by one of the strong men – usually my brother Mike – into the lean-to back kitchen where it would stand for about a week.

My mother told me that if a very large pig was slaughtered and it weighed about twenty stone it would be hung up in one of the elm trees that lined the lane leading to the cottage instead of hung on a ladder.

While the pig was in the back kitchen we children would be frightened to go out there especially at night time. We had to go through the back kitchen to get to the bathroom and I can remember frequently asking someone to stay by the bathroom door to see me safely back into the main part of the cottage.

After about ten days Hans the slaughterman would call one evening to cut up the pig and prepare it for curing and keeping.

A long wooden bench called a pig bench would have been scrubbed and made ready for use. The pig would be cut up and the sides of bacon laid onto the bench. Each side of bacon was salted and the joints would have a special salt applied called Salt Peter.

This was always a very busy time, especially for mother, melting down lard and making faggots.

From time to time Dad would go out to the back

kitchen in the evening to check the curing and adding more salt to the bacon. Sometime later it would be cut up into smaller pieces.

Although the killing of the pig was a sad time, the whole family was always well fed on delicious pig meat and bacon for many of the coming months.

Nothing from the pig was wasted and my dad used to tell us that the only thing you can't eat from a pig is its squeal!

Oh, how I remember that squeal.

EXCURSIONS AND A TRIP
TO THE QUEEN'S CORONATION

In my childhood days, in order to get around from village to village, everyone in the family had a bicycle and we thought nothing of a two mile ride to catch a bus or train.

When we were younger, Mum and Dad would sometimes take my sister and me to Gloucester on the train from Dymock to go to the Cinema. This would not happen very often but when it did it was a wonderful excursion. A highlight of the trip would be calling at Ye Old Fish Shoppe, a lovely old black and white building in Hare Lane in the city centre, where we would sit upstairs in the restaurant with a plate of fish and chips, bread and butter and a glass of lemonade. Then it was off to see the film and back home on the train to Dymock to collect our bikes.

Some Saturdays, when I was in my early teens, I would go on my own on the train to Gloucester to do some shopping for my mother. This was quite a responsibility for a young girl but it made me feel very grown up and it was always enjoyable. I had to ride my bike to Dymock to catch the train and would leave it at the railway station. I used to love stopping at the little stations on the way to Gloucester.

On some occasions I would travel on the bus from

Dymock leaving my bike with a lady we knew who lived in one of the council houses near the cricket ground. The bus came from Ledbury and would go to Newent and then on to the villages of Taynton, Tibberton and Highnam before arriving at Gloucester.

George Green (Caterers) Ltd.

Ye Olde . . .
Fish Shoppe

th Century   Phone: 22502

½ CHICKEN AND CHIPS ...... 6d.
COLD HAM + CHIPS - - - 2/9
CORNISH PASTIE AND CHIPS   2/3d.

Roe and Chips	2/6d.
Plaice and Chips	3/6d.
Steak and Kidney Pie and Chips	2/6d.
Fish and Chips	2/6d.
Fish Cake and Chips	1/6d.
Faggot, Chips and Peas	2/6d.
Egg and Chips	1/9d.
Sausages and Chips	2/-
Egg, Sausages and Chips	3/-
Egg, Sausage, Chips, Tomatoes and Beans	3/6d.
Peas	6d.
Baked Beans	6d.
Tomatoes	6d.
Bread and Butter	4d.
Tea (per cup)	5d.
Coffee	8d.
Minerals	8d.

Days and Times of opening:

Tues., Wed., Thurs. and Fri., 11.30 a.m. - 2 p.m., 4.30 - 11 p.m.
Sat., 11.30 a.m. - 2 p.m. and 4 - 7.30 p.m.

Minerals supplied by Davies Brook and Co. Ltd., Hereford

An old menu from the time when my family used to visit Ye Old Fish Shoppe. A plate of fish and chips then cost 2/6d which is 12½p in today's money! In comparison chicken and chips was expensive at 6/9d; chicken was quite a luxury in those days. On a recent visit to Gloucester I was delighted to discover that the fish and chip shop was still open with its upstairs restaurant very much as I remember it from over sixty years ago.

Another attraction in the winter time was the weekly film show at Brooms Green Village Hall. Usually all the kids from the village would walk there and back. The Laurel & Hardy films were always popular and there were many cowboy films which pleased the boys. Quite often the film projector would break down during the films which brought about a great cheer from the young audience. We would usually stop on the return home to buy a packet of crisps from the off-licence at The Horsehoe Inn.

There was also a kids' club held at the village hall called Kings Messengers which we occasionally went to. This was run by the vicar of Dymock Revd Gethyn-Jones and some of his helpers one of whom I recall was Mrs Daniels from Donnington Court Farm.

A great source of excitement was the October Fair in Ledbury. After school we would set off on our bikes to Greenway Halt to catch the train to Ledbury. The trains were pulled by small steam locomotives and we loved the smell of the steam and smoke and the sound they made as they chuffed along the country line to Ledbury. We would have a wonderful night at the Fair and then catch the return train to Greenway and cycle home.

I think my longest excursions as a young girl were when I went to London to stay with my Auntie Phyllis and Uncle Charles. My aunt was one of my mother's sisters and they lived near Wembley with my cousin Angela. Whenever they came to stay at Moors Cottage they would sometimes take me back with them.

As a young girl from the country I always remember on my first visit having difficulty getting to sleep with the distant roar of the traffic. It was always quite an experience going into London using the underground stations with their massive escalators. I saw many of the sights of London and the big shops but the most exciting trip was when we went to London as a family in June 1953 when I was nine years old.

This was the occasion of Queen Elizabeth's Coronation and my parents took my sister Sandra and me to London to stay with my aunt and uncle. We were thrilled to be able to watch the whole coronation on their television – a rare treat because we had no television back home in Ryton. My uncle at that time worked as a Clerk of the Works for the City of London and was involved in the setting up of the seats and decorations along the route taken by the Queen's Parade to Westminster Abbey and back to Buckingham Palace. He and my aunt were allocated seats in The Mall and had a wonderful time staying on into the evening to see the firework display. They told us the atmosphere was electric and the crowds unbelievable.

A few days after the coronation the Queen visited various districts around London and I remember standing on the side of the street near my aunt and uncle's house waiting for the Queen to drive by and waving my Union Jack as she passed.

What an experience for us as a simple country family coming up to London for such an occasion from our sleepy little Gloucestershire village.

In our nearby town of Newent there was a small cinema and I remember all the children from my Primary School were taken by bus to see the film of the Coronation. I felt very proud to be able to tell my friends that I was in London at the time and actually saw the Queen.

It was not only my family that enjoyed excursions. We had relatives who were scattered over different parts of the country, many of them living in cities such as London and Birmingham and they frequently visited us at Moors Cottage. Although our home was a very simple country cottage and a huge contrast to their city and urban life, they all enjoyed their visits whether for the day or for short holidays. My mum was a great homemaker and they were always made welcome and well looked after.

What was particularly exciting for us was that many of them had cars, which was a luxury we did not have, and they would often take us on drives around the countryside and to visit other relatives living nearby.

I have previously mentioned the food rationing which existed in the years following the War and this was something which had a significant effect on the day to day living of my relations living in the towns and cities. I remember as a girl they never went home empty handed. My dad was generous and they would leave with eggs, butter, bacon and pig meat to help out their limited rations back home. Country life did have advantages at that time.

ANIMALS ON CALLOW FARM

When my older brother, Mike, was still single and living at home he worked with my father on Callow Farm. They were always up very early in the mornings feeding the animals and doing their chores on our smallholding before going off to work for the day at The Callow.

Mr Chew had a lovely mixed farm of over three hundred acres with livestock and arable crops. There was a herd of pedigree Hereford cattle, a flock of sheep, pigs and of course the two working horses. Crops grown on the farm included corn, sugar beet, swedes, mangolds and grassland for the stock to graze and to make hay. The Callow, like most of the farms in the surrounding area, had the characteristic red sandy soil.

From time to time, when I was a young girl, Dad and Mike would allow me to go with them, usually in the afternoons, and I have some early memories of watching them working with the farm animals

In winter the cattle were housed in large cattle sheds with open yards to allow them to walk around outside during the day and go back in at night where they were bedded down on straw. The cattle had to be fed each day and their rations included hay, flaked maize, cattle cake and mangolds which had been grown on the farm. The hay was put into feeders in the open yards and the remaining food was put in mangers in the sheds. The cattle particularly enjoyed the mangolds and would munch away on these for hours. It was great fun going up into the haylofts to help push the hay down into the feeders. From the spring onwards the cattle were turned out into the fields to graze and the red and white Hereford cows with their calves were always a wonderful sight. We were always warned not to get close to the Hereford Bull.

The pigs were housed in a very big pig house and would make a terrible squealing noise when they knew it was getting near to feed time.

The sheep would stay out in the fields all year round. At lambing time the shepherd would build some large pens out of hurdles and surround them with bales of straw and the pregnant ewes would be put into these pens ready for lambing.

After lambing time the next two big tasks were shearing and dipping. This was always a busy time for the men on the farm and it was a question of 'all hands on deck'.

Shearing was carried out in one of the barns and the sheep were brought into one of the fields near the farm yard from where they were turned into a collecting pen in the barn ready to have their heavy woollen coats taken off. The shearing was originally done with hand clippers like large scissors but these were shortly to be replaced with a petrol shearing machine which drove mechanical clippers. The shearer would catch a sheep, usually a ewe, tip it up on to its rump and hold it firmly between his legs. He would them commence shearing the wool making sure he kept the fleece in one piece. The sheep would then be released and returned out to the field.

The fleeces were rolled up by other farmhands and put into large hessian sacks ready to be collected and taken away to the wool merchants.

When all the sheep had been shorn they were reunited with their lambs and a lot of bleating and crying would go on for quite a while whilst the lambs looked for their right mothers.

My dad always had soft hands at shearing time due to the lanoline in the wool.

After a few weeks the time for sheep dipping would come around.

The sheep dip was a large long concrete tank built into the ground, the bottom of which sloped up from a deep end to a shallow end. There was a gate at each end where the sheep would enter and leave, several at a time. The tank was filled with water into which a special sheep dip chemical had been added.

Some of the farm hands would gather the sheep from a nearby collecting pen and push them one at a time into the dipping tank where another workman, usually my father, would submerge them in the liquid using a special crook and push them through to the shallow end where they would scramble up a slope and out through the exit gate on to dry land. They would then have a good shake before returning to the field to graze away happily after their rather frantic ordeal.

Dad and my brother did not look forward to shearing and dipping because they were long hard days often done in hot weather. They were always thankful to come home at the end of each day and have a really good wash. If they were lucky they could have a bath but only if the old copper in the back kitchen had been lit to provide plenty of hot water.

Apart from the cattle, sheep and pigs, I have childhood memories of some other animals which could be seen crossing the fields– these were the horses and hounds of the local Hunt. To us children the hounds and riders on horseback were a lovely sight particularly the huntsmen in their red jackets. It was very much part of the country scene. The hunt would sometimes meet in the field above Quabbs Wood at the back of our cottage, and so we would be close to the hounds and riders. The hounds always seemed very friendly and would come up to us, jump up and lick our faces. They were so excited and ready for their day's hunting. Keeping them under control was quite a task for the whipper-in but he knew them all by name.

When it was time for them to move off the huntsman would blow his hunting horn and off they would go with all the riders following on horseback.

The hunting usually happened in the week and started before we left for school. It was always a disappointment when we had to leave and go off down the lane to catch the school bus.

If we were lucky we would sometimes catch sight of the hunt from the bus, galloping over the fields of Callow Farm making their way up to Ryton Woods where they would then ride on through Ketford Woods and away for the day, whilst we children went off to school.

TRADESMEN CALL

In my childhood days, living in the country had its advantages as well as its disadvantages. For one thing there didn't seem to be so much hustle and bustle with shopping – particularly food shopping – as there is today.

Most of the groceries, fresh bread and meat were delivered to us at the cottage. Bread deliveries were made by Fawke's Bakery in Dymock and there was nothing like the smell of freshly baked bread in their bread vans. Sometime later I recall bread being delivered by Fortys of Kempley and this was possibly after Fawkes Bakery closed. The local butcher John Gwatkin made a regular delivery of meat on a Saturday. I recall his shop was just below Ann Cam school in Dymock. Groceries were delivered weekly. Each Monday my mother would write out her grocery order in a notebook which was collected by the bread man when he next called, who then took it back to Mr Fawkes' grocery and bakery shop in Dymock. The order was delivered a few days later.

When the groceries arrived the butter came in one big slab wrapped in greaseproof paper. Sugar and currants were packed in blue bags – none of the fancy packaging and labelling that there is today.

However something that still looks the same as it did in those days are tins of Golden Syrup. When I was small, just after the end of the War, I remember there being a large tin of Tate & Lyle Golden Syrup kept in the pantry under the stairs. How mother came by it I do not know but I still remember the delight of getting a teaspoon and disappearing into the pantry to help myself to this lovely sweet treacle. Today I still cannot resist the temptation when making cakes to have a teaspoon of Golden Syrup. It's a wonder all my teeth have not fallen out!

The man who collected the money for the groceries was Mr Ken Causon who lived in Dymock near The Crown Inn. Ken was a real character and was a mine of information. Our house was usually his last call of the day and he would arrive fairly late in the evening and stay for a drink and a chat, telling us all the news and local gossip. I was usually sent to bed but could hear his voice in the living room and my mum's infectious laugh as he told his tales. Sometimes it was nearly midnight before he left to make his way home. I am sure his wife wondered why he was always home so late on Saturdays but as he stopped for a chat at each of his calls it was no wonder he arrived so late at our cottage. He seemed to enjoy the late hours and was never in a rush.

There was a milkman who delivered milk and papers to the village and he would leave our newspaper in a drainpipe at the bottom of the lane and it was collected each day by whoever was passing.

Coal and coke for the cooking range was delivered by Hyetts, Coal Merchants of Newent. For our Tilley lamps there was a separate delivery of paraffin.

Our other delivery was the post. The postman made his

deliveries of letters and parcels from Dymock post office where the mail had arrived by train at Dymock railway station and taken down to the post office ready to be sorted and delivered. With his sack on his back and large bag on the front of his bicycle he would make his deliveries and make collections at the same time from the post boxes on his way – summer and winter whatever the weather.

The River Leadon which meandered through the fields from Dymock, through Ryton and on to Ketford, would frequently flood during the winter months. When this happened it was impossible to ride a bicycle to catch a train or bus from Ryton and even get through to collect provisions from the local grocery store in Dymock. If the floods got too bad and the delivery vans were unable to get through, my dad would get the tractor and trailer from the farm and drive to Dymock to collect all the groceries for the village folk.

In the summer months we would occasionally get an ice cream van passing the bottom of Sandy Lane on its way from Dymock to Ryton. I remember we would wait at the bottom of the lane hoping he would turn up.

From time to time we would need to call the doctor if anyone in the family was ill. Our doctor's surgery was in Newent but because of our remote location the doctor would always give us a house visit if we were unable to get to the surgery.

Looking back I am reminded that despite the remoteness of our cottage we were very well catered for and my mother always had a well stocked pantry.

SUNDAYS AND WINTER EVENINGS

As children we were always encouraged to help with the cooking and baking. Sundays were always busy in the kitchen – mother cooking dinner and my sister and I making cakes and puddings. It seemed to be a tradition that whatever else was cooked for Sunday lunch there was always a rice pudding cooked in the range oven for Dad.

When not working in the kitchen with mother I would often go out on the smallholding with my dad and brother. There were always jobs to be done outdoors – building cow sheds, mending fences, repairs to pig sties, etc. This was very enjoyable and a great chance to be with my father who in the week was a very busy man with his work on the farm as well as back at home.

Sometimes on a Sunday afternoon Dad would take me to visit his father who lived at Upleadon. This would be about a twelve mile round trip and was a very long hard ride. I enjoyed these outings but often got very tired on the way home.

When we got to granddad's house I was apprehensive about going indoors because he had a housekeeper who could not speak properly due to her false teeth which were loose and kept falling down when she spoke. This used to put the wind up me a bit. Nevertheless she was always kind and we always had a cup of tea and cakes before looking around the garden and setting off on our long trek home.

I cannot remember my sister ever coming on these jaunts – I think she was too young being three years my junior.

Most Sunday mornings at about midday a neighbouring farmer Jack Rees from Ketford would walk up the lane on his way for a Sunday pint at The Horse Shoe Inn, Brooms Green. He would always stop to have a chat with Mum and Dad.

Sometimes I would wander down to Arty and Doris Taylor at Stream Barn Cottage where they lived with their two daughters Topsy and Betty and their son Ron. These three ladies taught me how to knit which was to become a favourite pastime of mine.

Another Sunday afternoon cycle ride was to Donnington. Some of the village girls and I would ride out to Donnington Court Farm to see the three Daniels boys – Francis, Ken and Robert – and they would join us on their bikes just riding up and down the lanes generally doing nothing in particular as kids do.

Sometimes on Sunday evenings in the summer my sister and I would be taken by our mum and dad to one of the local pubs for a drink. We would either walk along the lane to the Horseshoe Inn or ride our bikes to the Bell Inn at Bromesberrow Heath. The children would play on the lawns while the grownups sat inside the pub with the locals for a chat. They would buy us a bottle of pop and a bag of Smiths crisps and I remember it was good fun looking for the little blue bag of salt which we would untwist and shake all over the crisps. We were never late going home but these simple things in life were always a great treat and will always stick in my mind.

Sunday papers were delivered to one of the houses on the other side of the village and my sister and I would take it in turns to ride our bikes to collect these from Joe Williams at Gallows Cottage. Joe was a very happy jovial chap and he was a great tease. Sometimes he would stand in his garden looking across the fields to our cottage and if he saw my mother in our garden he would shout to her across the valley, 'Hello, Lollipop,' – her name was Laura and this was his nickname for her – 'are you alright?' She would shout back, 'Hello, Joe, yes, we are.' He was great fun and very often came to help Dad do odd jobs on the holding.

In later years when I was in my early teens some of the girls in the village and I used to ride our bikes to Dymock which was about two miles away to help swell the numbers in the choir at St Mary's Church. The choir gave the congregation a bit of a boost in the hymn singing. How good our voices were I am not sure. This trip would be repeated on Friday evenings for choir practice.

On reflection I am not sure whether our enthusiasm for choir practice was so much to do with singing or the attraction of the boys in the choir.

Winter months on the smallholding made jobs a lot harder for my dad and brother. There were all the animals which still needed feeding and cleaning and also the cow needed milking morning and night.

In order to see what they were doing at night they used to

carry Tilley lamps from shed to shed. These lamps gave out a good light and made a loud hissing noise all the time they were alight. We had about four Tilley lamps and also some oil lamps all of which had to be cleaned and primed before use. It was my mother and brother who usually did this each day. The lamps were cleaned and filled with paraffin and from time to time the wicks needed trimming and new mantles fitted. All these tasks were time consuming but were all in a day's work.

During the winter, the evenings would drag and I would get bored. We had no television in those days. At the end of the week my mother would often take me to the other side of the village to visit some of my friends. This was about one mile away and it was not a journey I could make on my own in the dark. Friday was usually the evening we went out to visit as there was no school next day.

Mother and I would wrap up in our big warm coats, hats and gloves and off we would go, each carrying a torch.

The houses we were heading for were either Gallows Cottage, where my friend Heather lived or Lime Tree Villa where my friend Wendy and her brothers and sisters lived. Mum was friendly with both families so the trips were enjoyable for us both.

Heather lived with her parents Joe and Frances Williams and her younger brother Duncan. Joe worked at The Callow with Dad. There was never a dull moment when we were there. When I was sixteen I was bridesmaid at Heather's wedding.

At Lime Tree Villa there was the large family of Gard and Marge Powell and their six daughters whose ages ranged from my own age up to teenagers and early twenties together their two older brothers. We girls would all spend many happy hours playing games together or even just huddled around the big open fire.

I can still visualise Marge Powell sat with a basket of Blenheim apples peeling and slicing them for us all to eat as we chatted around the log fire.

Walking the lanes on a clear frosty moonlight night was something special – the stars too numerous to count – and we used to stop to see if we could see the North Star or the Plough or even the Seven Sisters. Very occasionally in the clusters we would see a shooting star.

After a while our eyes would get used to the darkness and we would often walk back home by moonlight not needing our torches – the silence broken only by the hoot or screech of an owl.

BICYCLES AND LIFTS TO WORK

Most of the folk who lived in the village had bicycles. A few had motor bikes and in the early days just one family had a car.

Bicycles were very much an essential means of transport in those days. Before my sister and I were old enough to have our own bikes we would ride with our parents. My mother's bike was a ladies 'sit up and beg' which had a child's seat behind the saddle where Mum would sit my sister Sandra when she was a toddler. I was a few years older so I would sit on my dad's bike on a small saddle attached to the cross bar.

Our bikes were used to get us to and from other villages and to local shops of which there were several in the area. My mother would sometimes ride her bicycle to the post office and shop at Bromesberrow Heath which was at the cross roads in the village centre on to the road leading up to the Grove House. This was either to get a few provisions or to buy a postal order which she would use for the payment of anything she had ordered by post and the postal order was used instead of a cheque.

I too would quite often cycle to another small shop in

Bromesberrow Heath which was just before the post office
opposite the little lane leading to the Haffield road. This was
usually to buy sweets or the big round pink balls of bubble
gum which were all the rage at the time. We kids would
also ride to a tiny shop in Brooms Green just beyond the
Horseshoe pub where again we could buy sweets. Further
along from Brooms Green there was a small post office at
Greenway where I would occasionally ride to for a change.

Our bicycles enabled my family to get to a bus or
train to Ledbury or Gloucester. This would involve a two
mile cycle ride to Dymock where we would catch a bus
by the cricket ground or a train from the railway station.
Alternatively we would make a trip to the main Ledbury to
Gloucester road beyond Bromesberrow Heath where there
was a bus shelter at what was known as Letter House. We
would leave our bikes at the back of the bus shelter and
catch the bus. Our quickest route to the main Gloucester
road from Ryton was along Horse Croft Lane which was
off the Redmarley road.

The village policeman from Dymock was often to be
seen riding his bicycle along the roads around Ryton and he
would frequently stop and pass the time of day with locals. I
am sure he knew most of what was happening on his patch.

The local postman delivered the mail on his bicycle and
even the district nurse from Dymock cycled to make her
visits and deliver babies.

During the summer school holidays many of us girls
would cycle three or four miles to go blackcurrant picking.
We would cycle to the nearby village of Bromesberrow to
the currant fields between the main road and the village
school. We would set off early in the morning to get to

the fields for a full day's picking. It was usually very hot weather and we needed to take food and plenty of drinks with us. After a busy and tiring day we would set off to ride back home arriving worn out ready for a good night's sleep to set us up for the next day.

Another farm where we sometimes went picking was out on the Newent road just beyond Castletump. This was too far to ride our bicycles so the farmer would send a tractor and covered trailer to collect the pickers and then take them back home at the end of the day.

Blackcurrant picking was a very messy job but we could earn a nice few pounds during the few weeks that the work lasted.

It was such an inconvenience if your bike developed a puncture or broke down for one reason or another but thankfully my big brother would do the running repairs. He enjoyed tinkering and as long as he was not too busy doing maintenance on his motorbike there was usually no problem in attending to our bikes.

Mending a puncture was quite a fiddly job. With the help of a few spoon handles the tyre was prised from the rim of the wheel and the inner tube removed. This tube was then pumped up and held under a bowl of water until bubbles appeared. Once the hole in the tube was located the tube was dried and some white powder chalk smoothed over the hole to completely dry it and to mark the spot where a repair patch was then stuck. Once this had been done and the adhesive had dried the tube was put back in the tyre and the tyre carefully prised back on to the wheel. Hopefully when the tyre was inflated it would stay up and all would be well.

Some of the girls from the village cycled to Dymock Church on Sunday evenings to help swell the choir and sometimes one of us would be called upon to pump the bellows on the church organ. The church services were fairly well attended in those days but was always full to overflowing at harvest and other festivals.

When I left school aged fifteen and went to work in the nearby town of Ledbury, over four miles away, my bicycle was essential. Most of the girls in our village had jobs in the town and we cycled together to and from work. In the summer it was a pleasure but in the winter and in the rain it was not. When the weather was very bad with snow on the ground I can remember walking to work and back.

After a year or two the other girls got jobs elsewhere and I was the only one left travelling to Ledbury. I then started riding my bike to Greenway and leaving it at one of the cottages by the tiny post office. I would then catch the bus into Ledbury at Greenway Crossroads. When the lady moved from the cottage I arranged to leave my bike with Mrs Bennion at the Stone House on the cross roads.

At that time I worked for the local firm of auctioneers who sold livestock in Ledbury Market. Sometimes the cattle lorry drivers would stop and give me a lift to work. They knew me because they often collected animals from home to take them to Gloucester Market. I can remember once having a lift in the fire engine on its way back to the Fire Station after attending a fire. In those days there was not a lot of traffic on the roads and most of the people travelling knew one another which was very useful at times. I must say it was not always easy climbing up into the cab of a lorry with skirts and high heels but somehow I managed.

After about four years cycling to and from work I changed my job and was fortunate to get a position at the local telephone exchange as a G.P.O. telephonist. This involved different working hours so I went to lodge with some German friends of our family, Hans and Margaret, who had moved from nearby Knights Green to a new house in Knapp Close, Ledbury. At weekends I went back home to Moors Cottage.

My bicycle did not become completely redundant because a couple of years later I had started courting and my boyfriend Jim would come out to our cottage most weekends and we would enjoy going off on cycle rides. That was before he passed his test and had his first car – a split windscreen Morris Minor.

What luxury!

THE NIGHTINGALE WOOD

Moors Cottage stood in an elevated spot between two little country lanes. The one was called the Back Lane which ran behind our cottage and was a pedestrian access to Quabbs Cottage and Stream Barn Cottage and then continued over a ford and wooden footbridge on out to the village. The other we called the front lane although its proper title was Sandy Lane which ran down between high sided sandy banks and led to the village.

When I was a young girl the back lane was very damp, muddy and boggy and was only used by pedestrians. Sandy Lane in contrast was very dry and sandy with grass growing up the middle. It was used by most people on their bikes, motorbikes or the occasional car and of course it was also used by the horses making their way to working on the land.

Our kitchen garden gate led into the back lane and immediately opposite was another gate leading into a field which ran down to a most magnificent wood we called The Quabbs, although I believe its proper name was Quabbs Coppice. This wood was home to lots of wildlife and many birds including Nightingales. On many an early summer's evening just as it was getting dusk, my father would call us out of the house to listen to the beautiful song of the Nightingale. We would just stand there looking down on the wood listening to its lovely rich melody.

In The Quabbs there were carpets of wild daffodils for which this part of the world is renowned. When the daffodils had finished flowering the whole wood was carpeted in bluebells – such a wonderful sight.

The wood had beautiful black peaty soil which was so different to the red sandy soil found in the surrounding fields. Decades of leaf mould must have contributed to this rich dark soil. In the wood it was quite boggy and my father used to call the woodland floor 'quabby' because he said the word quab meant boggy or marshy ground. I remember there was a spring on the back boundary of the wood and a stream running from the spring down the side of the wood and on across the fields towards Quabbs Cottage and beyond.

The Quabbs wood also provided a great source of sport and entertainment for the young men in the village who used to go rabbiting nearly every Sunday afternoon. My brother would take our terrier dog, one of the other lads would bring the ferrets and off they would go for many hours. Sometimes I was allowed to go with them but being so much younger I am sure it was only under sufferance. Some days they would catch lots of rabbits with some to share out and other days none at all. If there were any left over they would take them to the local butcher Mr John Gwatkin in Dymock for him to sell in his shop. During and after the War, with strict meat rationing, these rabbits provided a good supply of fresh meat to feed the family and would supplement the meat rations. Unfortunately when the disease myxomatosis (or mixy as my dad and brother called it) arrived the rabbits began to die in their hundreds. This was a most awfully cruel disease and from then on many people would not eat rabbit.

In the winter months our mother would take my sister and I down to The Quabbs to collect firewood which was usually fallen dead branches. This job was usually done on the weekends. We had a 'dilly' which was a wooden box on four pram wheels towed by a rope and this would be filled with the firewood and dragged back up to the cottage.

I remember the time when it was murmured in the village that Quabbs wood was going to be felled and cleared and integrated into the adjoining fields to grow corn. In one of my earlier stories I mentioned that when the Water Authority sunk a new bore hole in Bromesberrow Heath many of the wells in the area went dry. We were told that one of the other consequences of this work was to cause the wet boggy ground in The Quabbs to drain and dry out. Gradually the ground began to sink exposing the tree roots and in time this caused many of the trees to die. In the end there was little for it but to have the wood felled and cleared.

Naturally we were all very upset about this but nothing could be done and the inevitable day arrived when the wood was felled. I well remember seeing all the old tree stumps being burned. It was so sad – all the wildlife – all the flowers – all the birds – the nightingales – all gone from their natural habitat.

For years to come, although ploughed and sown with corn, the black soil where the wood once stood could still be seen standing out from the red sandy soil of the surrounding land.

How much we missed that beautiful wood. To us there was no other wood in the locality like The Quabbs and no other melody like the song of the nightingale.

LATER YEARS

Moors Cottage was my home for over twenty one years but in 1966 it was time to move on. Jim and I got married in April of that year and settled into our new bungalow in Ledbury. However Mum and Dad continued to live at the cottage for another twelve years during which time Jim and I, and later with our two children Helen and Stephen, would visit them most weekends. Jim loved going out to help Dad with the animals and the children loved the freedom of playing there. That is when I was prompted to start writing these stories of my own childhood in Ryton.

In 1978 something happened which was to be a life changing event for my parents. Mr Chew decided to retire and sell Callow Farm but before doing so he approached Dad to see if he would be interested in purchasing Moors Cottage which Dad had rented from him for over forty years. By this time Dad had been retired for several years through ill health and my parents had already been wondering where they might have to move to if they could no longer look after the smallholding.

I am pleased to say agreement was reached with Mr

CALLOW FARM
RYTON   DYMOCK   GLOS.
Gloucester 15 miles, Dymock 2 miles, Newent 5 miles, Ledbury 5 miles, M50 (Junction 2) 2 miles

in conjunction with

C. T. & G. H. SMITH

are instructed by Messrs. A. H. Chew & Son to
SELL BY AUCTION
on
FRIDAY, 14th APRIL, 1978
at 12 NOON (under cover)

The Callow Herd of
100 ACCREDITED PEDIGREE HEREFORDS

comprising 46 cows and heifers (the majority with calves at foot), 29 maiden heifers (11 18—24 months and 18 10—18 months) and the 2 STOCK BULLS

30 HEREFORD STORE CATTLE
(steers and heifers 10—20 months)

150 BREEDING EWES
AND THEIR LAMBS
(130 Clun ewes, 20 Suffolk cross Clun tegs) and 2 RAMS (Suffolk and Hampshire)

IMPLEMENTS and MACHINERY
including 1974 FORD 4000 and 2 DEXTA TRACTORS, MF baler, Ransome mower, Stanhay root drill, Ransome 3-furrow plough, Parmiter beet elevator, Lister bale elevator, Perry bale loader, Cambridge roll, cultivators, trailers, etc., 3-phase Grain auger, POLDENVALE SHEEP HANDLING EQUIPMENT and COMMODORE SHEEP HANDLER

LICENSED CATERING APPLIED FOR

Catalogues and further details from Bruton, Knowles & Co., The Cattle Market, Gloucester. Tel. (0452) 33441 and Messrs. C. T. & G. H. Smith, New Street, Ledbury, Hfds. Tel. 2388

Poster of the sale of Live and Dead Farming Stock at Callow Farm in 1978 on behalf of A. H. Chew & Son, following the sale of the farm. Bruton Knowles of Gloucester dealt with the auction in conjunction with my husband's firm C. T. & G. H. Smith of Ledbury.

Chew and Dad was able to purchase the cottage with its farm buildings and some of the small fields totalling about one and three quarter acres. Mr Chew then took back the remaining few acres of land which Dad had previously rented.

Shortly after the property had been purchased Dad's health deteriorated and he could no longer look after the stock and do the work on the holding. The thought of leaving Moors Cottage was hard to contemplate but both Mum and Dad agreed that they could not stay there and see it deteriorate. They had always prided themselves on keeping it neat and tidy. The decision was made to move into Ledbury and they were able to sell the cottage and purchase a small bungalow in Birch Close, near to my sister and me.

Sadly, Dad did not live to enjoy the bungalow for more than a few months and he passed away in the summer of 1979. Mum really enjoyed her new life in Ledbury and made lots of friends. She continued to live in the bungalow for over twenty years before she passed away in 2000.

In the meantime a huge change took place in my life which was to take me and the family away from the place of my youth to a completely unknown part of the country over two hundred miles away. Jim had been contemplating a change in his career and in 1982 an opportunity arose with a firm of agricultural auctioneers in Truro, Cornwall where a new livestock market had just been built. So we took the plunge and made the move. We were then to spend thirty very happy years in the county of Cornwall surrounded by the sea and lovely beaches which we all enjoyed. In due course the children left school and eventually their education and work took them out of Cornwall – Helen to Surrey as a teacher and Stephen eventually back to Ledbury as a landscape gardener.

Just after Jim retired I had some health problems and the children felt that it would be better if we moved back to be closer to them and to do so whilst we were still active enough to make the move and settle into a new way of life.

In 2013 we said goodbye to Cornwall and moved back to Herefordshire to a bungalow in the delightful village of Much Marcle, near Ledbury.

For Jim and I the move back to the Ledbury area was very much a case of returning to our roots and now I am living just a few miles from my childhood home.

Sadly my sister Sandra and my brother Mike had by then passed away and I am now the only remaining member of our little family that grew up in Ryton. I have dedicated this book in memory of them all.

One big thrill for me is that our new home is on the edge of my beloved wild daffodil country on the doorstep of what is now famously known as the Golden Triangle where the villages of Kempley, Oxenhall and Dymock hold their popular and much visited Daffodil Weekends.

Here visitors and local people alike can enjoy these lovely native flowers of Gloucestershire in their natural habitats of meadows and woodlands as well as along the verges and hedgerows of the lanes and by-roads.

Each spring since moving back to Much Marcle, Jim and I have once again been able to enjoy the magnificent seasonal displays of wild daffodils and I have been able to soak up the beauty of the flowers of my childhood days.

We also love driving around the area where I was brought up and of course visiting Ryton and passing by my old home.

The lane leading up to Moors Cottage has now been surfaced with tarmac and no longer has its sandy tracks with the grass strip up the middle but to me it will always be Sandy Lane.